How I got fit
by learning to swim

From zero to race

Antonio Loglisci

Title: HOW I GOT FIT BY LEARNING TO SWIM

Copyright © 2014 by Antonio Loglisci

First Printing: 2014

ISBN: 978-1-291-97668-7

www.swim-fit.com

DEDICATION

For my mother,
who swims only with a lifebuoy…

For my father,
who swims only where his feet touch the ground…

For my brother,
who has been swimming forever.

Dedicated to all those for whom:
"It is never too late"

ACKNOWLEDGMENTS

This book exists because I had the fortune to receive the right tools to transcribe some events in my life in a useful and interesting way. These tools, rigorously delivered in a rightful tool chest, have been given to me by an exceptional individual, and meeting him has changed my life for the better. This individual, whose job is to awaken souls with the power of awareness is my dear friend Claudio, better known as Professor Claudio Sante Cavalieri d'Oro. My first acknowledgment is for him, who, by educating me passed on the Evolution, that extraordinary shaping event dedicated to Evolving and Giving Value to personal and team Potential.

This book exists also because I have a person by my side that has always supported me, encouraged me and pushed me to write, joking with a sentence that has become my torment: on what page are you? This person's name is Claudia Fazzi, my wonderful life companion who, in addition to having given me the right motivations to win my professional and sports challenges, has drawn all the illustrations in this book, and I think that they are the cutest sketches in the world.

Lastly, special thanks go out to Marco and Ivano, the two coaches who helped me become a good swimmer.

CONTENTS

INTRODUCTION

In this August night, as I lay in a hotel bed immersed in darkness, I had only one hope: I hoped to be able to sleep. As it turns out, my wish was not granted, as I had been trying in vain to fall asleep for hours. I was suspended in a state between wake and sleep, much like a car hanging at the edge of a cliff. Every time I was about to enter the world of dreams, an involuntary muscle contraction set me back into motion, making me lose my state of relaxation.

It was all nerves, no doubt. I could do nothing else but think of what will happen tomorrow morning. And as soon as my brain envisioned the exciting scenes that awaited me, my heart began to gallop, making me feel awake and alert. I tried to think of other things; to recall relaxing images of alpine lakes, mountain landscapes and starry skies, but after a few minutes of successful escapes, everything went suddenly back to the way it was before. If that weren't enough, the bed was too soft, the pillow was too high and the doors of the other rooms wouldn't quit slamming. In this

1

state of anticipation and anxiety, all that went on around me bothered me. I was certain that the following night everything would be over, and I would think back on those moments and smile. But not now.

Beee-beep, beee-beep, beee-beep, beee-beep! No, it can't be! Surely I must have made a mistake when I set the alarm. I looked down at my watch to check. Unfortunately there was no error in setting: it was 7 AM and time to get up. With the clear awareness of not having slept at all, I stood up and enjoyed the strange sense of vertigo that ran through my head. It vaguely reminded me of those times when I had one drink too many. Maybe I should sit down for a moment... now I was doing much better. I kissed Claudia to wake her and, with a little extra effort, I stood up again and slowly pulled up the rolling shutters, as if spying the weather conditions, hitting off a poker player who peeks at his cards: it had been raining on and off for days, and it would have been nice to see a little sunshine. I was blinded by the light of a gorgeous day, which confirmed that we would finally have a warm day.

Later, at the hotel's restaurant, I looked around and was surprised to see so many people in athletic suits intent at having breakfast. They were also here for the same reason as me, but their faces were relaxed, smiling and they almost looked amused. Just a few of them made an effort not to eat too many sweets and snacks. On closer observation, they looked more like students on a field trip than athletes gearing up for a swim meet. I observed them with curiosity, and I tried to assess if their behavior was a technique to release stress rather than real inner tranquility. Then I looked inward, and I couldn't help but notice that, although I came here just to have fun, inside lay a true tempest of emotions. Claudia, my sweet and sensitive companion who sensed my state of mind, tried to distract me by commenting on the quality of the food, the participants' congeniality and the athlete's bottomless stomach. I was not responding to her attempts.

We loaded our duffel bags and got in the car. I drove for about an hour before we reached our destination. The facility hosting the event was a large one, but its parking lot could barely hold half the vehicles of those attending. With a little luck, I found a tiny spot in between the other cars. I grabbed my bag and headed to the entrance. The barriers were high, tight, packed and they obstructed the view of what was happening inside the swim stadium. Only the fluttering of tall and colorful flags suggested that an international event was taking place inside. Besides, the loud buzz in the building reminded me of a stadium during a soccer match. At one point the buzz turned into rumble. My legs froze with emotion and they began to tremble. I heard the whistle being blown by an official, followed by the unmistakable metallic voice that pronounced the phrase: "Take your marks..." Beep! I couldn't see anything from my position; however, my heart seemed to have understood everything, as it began to pound inside my chest. My eyes were curious to uncover what was happening inside and, at the same time, I was a bit afraid. As if stabbing me in the back, a voice inside me whispered something strange and unexpected: "Now, why did you come to the European Masters' Championships?".

PREFACE

"If I did it, anyone can" – A. Loglisci

You are holding a very special book. Firstly because, although this is a book about swimming, it is not a swim manual. The purpose of a swim manual is to instruct the reader through accurate explanations on principles of technique, training and biomechanical and physiological processes, including an overview on rest and diet. Often times the author is a coach, an ex-swimmer or anyone who has in-depth knowledge in the field. I am not a major expert of this sport, therefore I could not write a manual. I learned to swim as an adult, often turning to the art of managing. I had to first tackle the limits set by learning at an advanced age and then course teachings that were not always in line with the participants' expectations. Thus, what you'll find here is the original viewpoint of an individual who learned to swim attending courses after work. For this reason you will like my stories, because if you are a swimmer, you will find them similar to what you do, while if you are still not a swimmer, you will have the opportunity to get to know something that goes beyond the sport and that has something to do with the way human beings react and think.

Is this a psychology book? Although that subject is touched upon repeatedly, this is not a psychology book. Personally I read several books about that discipline, and I had the opportunity to observe how some of them are truly useful to improve the life of individuals over a short period of time; that is why, although I do not discuss theory, in these pages you will have the opportunity to get to know principles and effects of some of the traditional tools of Neuro-Linguistic Programming and Transactional Analysis, which I have found helpful in producing interesting results over a short period of time.

Another important thing is that, while you read, you will have fun, although this is not a humorous book. It is my firm belief that the best way to reciprocate your interest is to allow you to enjoy your reading by making you smile, without forgetting the important fact: funny writing is easier to read, while boring writing can only make you go to sleep. That's the reason why my tales have a little ironic, nice and humorous slant, but remember one thing: behind a clown's mask lies a face that can be extremely serious. So behind the smiles aroused by my misadventures, all rigorously authentic, you will have the opportunity to learn some mental strategies that can come in handy.

So, if I really must place this book into a category, then I can say that it is a book about love; a book that tells of the burning passion that a human being has for the best and most ancient sport in the world: swimming.

INSTRUCTIONS FOR USE

Four in one

This book is broken down into ten chapters. Each chapter is made up of four parts; each part deals with swimming from a different point of view. In a certain way, it will almost seem like reading four books in one!

- **Experience** – The first part introduces the story of my learning.
- **Analysis** – Conversely, in the second part, you will find the analysis of my experience and the processing of mental strategies that have allowed me to reach results.
- **Emotion** – Exactly because the book is a love story, in this part you will find a passage that speaks directly to your heart.
- **Exercise** – Practice is worth more than grammar, so at the end of every chapter I suggest a simple exercise with which, if you want, you can take action.

A style as fluid as water

As my intention is to allow you to feel sensations similar to those that may be felt in the water, I tried to write in a way that:
- the lines may flow smoothly under your eyes;
- speaking to you informally, your contact with the content is fresh and direct;
- concepts appear transparent and immediately comprehensible.

Enjoy your reading,
Antonio Loglisci

CHAPTER 1: WHY SWIM?

EXPERIENCE - Why I began

As much as I always loved physical activity, I never became a real athlete until I was thirty years old. As a child, I sought fulfillment by chasing the sports dreams I held in my heart, but for one reason or another I never succeeded in specializing or becoming good at anything, so I never really experienced competitiveness in an official event.

It all began in the most ordinary way. As a child, like most Italian children, I dreamed of becoming a famous soccer player. It was the early eighties, and the stars that inspired us children's imagination were named Rumenigge, Paolo Rossi, Falcao, Antognoni, Maradona and Platini. Juventus FC won most of the championships, but when Italy won the World Cup, held in Spain in 1982, even the fans of other teams got to experience the joy of a collective celebration. Italian TV featured the first wave of Japanese cartoons, which, although filled with values (friendship, love, peace and loyalty) almost never proved to be educational. Do you want to contrast an alien invasion? Then you need an enormous robot equipped with rotating blades, space halberds and central missiles you have to arrest the advance of evil in the world? You special powers, high technology exoskeletons or a couple of large guns, like bazookas. Do you wish to become a famous soccer player? Then you must kick tree trunks and allow enormous tractor wheels to roll over your shinbones, otherwise you will never succeed in hitting a ball sufficiently hard to make it spin through the air, curve like a boomerang and transform into a ball of fire that can disintegrate the gloves of the opponent's goalie and turn them into ashes; the cartoon series "Here Come the Superboys" was pretty harsh. Compared to it, the "Holly and Benji" cartoons, which landed in Italy a few years later, were but a documentary.

The trouble is that no Italian child was busy winning the Japanese championship or the World Cup, so nothing on TV taught you anything truly useful to win your daily challenges, such as "getting picked" by a soccer team. Right, because in order to play for an amateur club, it is not enough to show up in shorts and sneakers on the field and very politely ask, "Excuse me, can I play with you?" There are more than enough children aspiring to become soccer players, while there are very few spots available.

And so when I was around seven years old, I attended my first tryout having no clue as to what this may mean. A few days later, after going to a couple of practices and some small matches with my district's team, I began to grasp the concept as my father said to me: "We won't be going to practice today." "What do you mean? They are expecting me!" I replied. And he, pulling from the bag of sweet lies, added, "The coach explained to me that there are too many 'dren in the position you want to play, so if you want to ne a regular, we'd better try out with another team." I ut with another team, and then another and then one 't I always obtained the same result: rejected! It's 'ms of soccer, I was a true failure. While on the field I covered areas that were a long way from the ball, where, far from anyone marking me, I ran freely back and forth, proving to everybody that, if nothing else, I did not lack effort or breath. From time to time, and not without hesitation, I raised my hand to ask for the ball, secretly hoping to never be taken seriously: the idea of finding myself with the ball between my feet and to have to do something about it terrorized me. When I didn't get picked up as a regular even by the church team, I reached the sad conclusion that maybe soccer was not the right sport for me.

At age 11, it was a school requirement for me to attend swim lessons for one year. This did not excite me at all because I did not love being in the water, except when taking a bath in the bathtub of my house. I was very thin and I immediately got cold. When we went to the beach, I was the first to get out of the water and sit to watch the others, asking myself how in the heck anyone could stay in the water for so long without freezing.

The most recurring humiliation I was subjected to as a child consisted of repeated showings of my childhood videos in front of family, friends and acquaintances. The most devastating one, which regularly exposed me to public ridicule, was the one depicting me being held by my father at the beach: he was laughing as, little by little, he dunked me into the salt water hoping to see me laugh with joy; I, on the other hand, cried, screamed and desperately grabbed his neck trying to reach the highest and safest place away from that cold, wet and unstable element, which I hated from the bottom of my soul. Therefore, the news of mandatory swim lessons at school did not sound enticing, at all. The only thing that I did enjoy was the half hour of warm up exercises that preceded getting in the water: as everyone was in their bathing suits, rubber shoes, t-shirt and white socks (in accordance with the rules), I could see my female classmates as I had never seen them before. However, when it was time to get in the water, I experienced deep feelings of anxiety. Even with the use of arm floats, a lifebuoy, kickboards and the presence of the instructor who held me by the arm, I truly could not relax and chase away that malevolent fear of drowning. When I found myself at the deep end, I constantly felt like I was dropping to the bottom, so I reacted by stiffening up and shaking out of control; this resulted in my drinking, drinking and drinking pool water as if I had been told to drain the pool. During my year of swim lessons, and luckily only one year was mandatory, I learned little and I got quite scared, developing considerable hatred of the pool.

Only a few years later, at the beach, while deflating my lifebuoy and trying to wear mask and snorkel, I again began experiencing a floating sensation to the extent that I started telling people that I had learned to swim. In reality, all I knew at the age of 13 were cannon balls, doggy paddle and some front crawl. In the end, what I learned is enough to live the normal life of a teenager in the city of Milan where, to define yourself a swimmer among your peers, all it takes is to know how to do these three things, as well as knowing how to swim to the sandbar at the Lido. As a popular vacation destination for many church youth groups from Milan, the Lido is a resort managed by the municipality, which contains two enormous pools filled with water shipped in from the North Pole. In the middle of the oval pool, right where your feet can't touch the ground, is a cement platform known as the oxbow, which can be reached by swimming for a few meters in the deep end. This represented a true proof of courage for a child of my age.

Since I was quite skillful at avoiding things I couldn't do, I succeeded in avoiding the oxbow for a very long time, using excuses such as: "It's just for little kids," "my leg hurts," "I don't feel like it" and so forth. Then one day during summer camp, I felt like the time had come for me to take on the oxbow. Not fearing failure, and holding a Tango brand ball close to my chest and saying "I'll take the ball to the sandbar so we can play there", I entered the water, and I began to kick my feet, trying to remain calm even when the water level began to rise. A few meters before arriving at the oxbow, my mind began to think of what could happen to me if the ball slipped away from my hands. The panic took over and my stomach tied up into a knot. I held the ball even tighter, and I kicked my feet with all my energy until, within a few seconds, I too arrived at the sandbar. For a moment I felt happy, but then I reconsidered the assistance provided by the ball, and I couldn't help but feel a little loss of personal pride because I was unable to get there relying solely on myself.

As the years went by, my sports experiences were easily summarized as: playing soccer with my classmates, playing soccer with my classmates during recess and playing soccer against other classes - which often turned into a brawl. Between the ages of 15 and 16, I finally made it into a team. A soccer team? No, a basketball team. In Italy, basketball is a secondary sport and so overshadowed by soccer that "making the team" does not involve any tryouts; all you have to do is pay the enrollment fee, show up at the court and train with the others. They set a clear condition for me: "Antonio, you still haven't fully learned the principles of this sport, so for one year you will have to be on the team with the younger boys, alright?" Surely, also because if, on one hand, I get to play in the same team as my cousin, on the other hand, even though I am just 5'6", I am much taller, beefier and much faster than my teammates, as they are two years younger than me and just approaching early adolescence. So everything worked out, right? Not even close, because the fact that I was in a different age group meant that I inevitably could not play in championship games, thus my participation was limited to practice and scrimmages. However, technically speaking, I didn't play too badly: I could dribble without losing control of the ball along the way, I passed the ball rather accurately and I had a fairly good field goal percentage. There is only one thing that partially lowered my performance: my aimlessly running back and forth as I had learned to do in soccer. Needless to say, doing just that is the best way to guarantee that you will be replaced by another player within a few minutes because you will soon be out of breath; and that is systematically what happened to me.

The following year, they moved me to the right team for my age group and my love for basketball began to fade. My teammates were all very tall and technically advanced. Not me. My teammates knew all their strategies by heart. Not me. The only thing for which I stood out was sprints. I was very quick at running without the basketball, and I was just as quick when it came to deciding to quit basketball when I had to be away from the court for a month for my appendectomy.

Between the ages of 16 and 20, my concept of sport became fitness, so I began lifting weights to stay in shape. By lifting weights my body stayed toned and in good health. But right when I began feeling satisfied because I found a good way to exercise, the tendons in my left elbow got incredibly inflamed causing a very bothersome epicondylitis, also known as "tennis elbow." I took care of it, but it continued to bother me for years, keeping me from physical strain. In addition to that, I was also affected by a couple of instances of inguinal hernia and another inflammation in my left knee.

The total package of medical issues lent a perfect alibi to stop doing any physical activity for at least seven years.

When I was little I enjoyed spending time envisioning what I would have done in the year 2000. It seemed to be a very distant date, out of reach, as if it would arrive only after waiting for an eternity. On the other hand, here I was in the new Millennium, at the age of 27. I had been working for a publisher for two years now; I led a pleasantly sedentary life and, nutritionally speaking, I enjoyed very elaborate lunches. The obvious consequence of everything I went through in the past is that, as time went by, I gained weight without realizing it. I was light years away from the "soccer star" I had dreamed of becoming. But things were about to change...

I was to undergo a medical examination for the first time since I had joined this company. The medical was arranged as a result of legal guidelines for the health and safety of workers, with which, even a simple programmer-operator like me must comply by participating in periodical testing. At the end of my medical, the doctor assumed a curious gloomy expression as he looked almost worried. He sighed deeply and then announced my test results as if they were those of a future heart patient: "Five feet, six inches... 159 pounds... size 38... you eat whatever..." Then, glaring at me as if he wanted to inflict the final blow, he asked the question I feared the most: "Listen, Loglisci, do you do any exercise?" I answered, "Well, you see... I quit. You know, there is never any time to exercise in between so many activities... plus I also have a partial bilateral inguinal hernia, so I can't even go to the gym..." At this point my life had taken a turn and things were about to change. "Loglisci, why don't you do some swimming? So you can unload some stress..." I didn't grasp the concept of unloading some stress, but as the word 'swimming' reached my ears, it was immediately processed as operating instructions to follow to a T. Without further delay, I got busy looking for swim lessons; overlooking the fact that I could barely float and, most of all, that I hated swimming pools with a passion!

ANALYSIS - Why you could start

In a recent study, ISTAT [Italy's National Statistics Institute] measured the popularity of various sports in our country. The study revealed that approximately three and one-half million people practice swimming, while four million practice soccer, Italy's most beloved sport. Upon closer analysis, we discover that the contingent of swimmers does not comprise a specific age group because, even though the largest age group is from 3 to 10 year olds, it is also true that the 11-19, 20-34 and 35-59 age groups are statistically very similar to one another. What is the meaning of all this? It means that from a statistical point of view, water activities are not just extremely widespread, but also loved by people of any age and social class. You probably already know the reasons for this: technique counts more than physical strength, practice takes place in absence of gravity so, from a traumatic point of view, there are no great stresses for the body. So, unless you have major health problems, nothing can keep you from becoming a swimmer throughout your entire life span. But this is something that, more or less, most people already know. What most people don't know, however, is that more and more amateurs enjoy taking their swimming to a competitive level at the Masters' class...

European Masters' Championships in Slovenia. I had a couple of hours before my freestyle event, so I was killing time by sitting on the stands and watching others competing. It's always fun to watch the homogeneity of the relays, as they are picked based on the participants' ages as well as years of experience. This is done so the swimmers can battle until the last meter without occurrences such as: the first ends their competition while the others are still halfway down the lane.

When it was time for the women's 50 meter butterfly event, the arena exploded in a spontaneous applause. Unfortunately I had left my eye glasses in the locker room, so I had to squeeze my eyes to get a glimpse of those swimmers, who were lined up for the start. I focused on approximately ten women who joyously saluted the crowd. They were all elderly, but the distance between us did not allow me to accurately estimate their age. Two of them had a hard time climbing on the starting blocks, but with a little effort they too reached their starting position. With a metallic voice, the starter announced: "Take your marks..." Beep! All ten swimmers dove in and they began swimming doing the butterfly. I admiringly observed their performance, which, rather than a competition looked more like a science experiment performed to prove that competitive swimming may be practiced at any age. There was no yield in their action, but only much grit and some technical expedients to successfully complete strenuous movements throughout the entire fifty meters. After approximately one minute, I saw them reach the wall and leap out of the water to peek at the timer; one among them made a gesture of elation and then, one by one, they exited the water and returned to the starting blocks to retrieve their slippers and robes. I watched them carefully to try to estimate how old they may be. By the time they walked by me, they were no longer wearing a cap so I had the opportunity to look over their faces, as well as their white hair. I watched them carefully and, for a moment, I had the clear sensation that my mind was struggling to process reality. I was thrilled when I realized that all those ladies were approximately eighty years old. They were joyous, smiling and their eyes shined with happiness. They looked like a bunch of little girls who just got off a carnival ride. My mind associated this scene with the movie Cocoon; in which a group of senior citizens recovered youth and energy by immersing themselves in the waters of a miraculous pool. I tuned into their conversations: some spoke English and German, while others spoke Swedish. I was speechless, and I thought of how I would like to be in similar physical shape when I reached that age...

As opposed to other sports, swimming is practiced in especially unique conditions because it requires your body to be completely immersed in a fluid. While in the water, the force of gravity acting on your body is approximately six times lower than that on dry land. Here's a detail not to be overlooked: humans naturally float in water. By Archimedes' principle, "A body immersed in a fluid is buoyed up by a force equal to the weight of the displaced fluid." Considering that the specific weight of the water is higher than that of the body because the latter holds air in its cavities, a human being, who before birth lives for all of nine months immersed in a liquid, is naturally geared to float. To test this, all you have to do is breathe in, hold your breath and immerse yourself in water (if you don't know how to swim, only do this when supervised by a swim instructor). Vice versa, in order for you to sink you must perform different and unnatural actions, as in, you must completely empty out your lungs, resist the consequent need for air and, lastly, allow yourself to slowly sink to the bottom. Alternatively, you must equip yourself with stabilizing masses or weights, like scuba divers do to explore sea bottoms.

Here's another true thing: floating requires a true act of faith. If you don't embrace it when you are in deep water, the instinctive part of your brain, drilled by a thousand pieces of danger information, takes over and activates an emergency maneuver by ordering all its muscles to contract rapidly and convulsively to allow you to grab a stable support. As it turns out, this is a betraying command because, in this way, all you can do is to grope, increasing the rate with which your stomach and lungs fill with water. Conversely, when you have faith in your buoyancy, it then comes natural to stop your brain's impulsive intervention and do exactly the opposite of what it tells you, starting to swim slowly, relaxing your nervous system and decontracting your muscles so their density decreases.

Another important thing is to eliminate the anguish caused by having water in your mouth. When you are immersed in water, it is quite normal for a little water to flow into your mouth, but, even if you swallow some (obviously in minimal quantities) this does not mean that you are starting to drown or that you will catch something from what you swallowed.

In addition to floating, true swimming requires the ability to move from one point to another in the water without setting foot on the bottom, if it were possible. When you swim, you are primarily propelled by arms and legs;

although, even your head and trunk contribute because the lack of contact with a solid surface allows for your movements to activate countless muscles and body parts. In other words, swimming makes your entire body move: this is the reason why it is considered the most complete and least traumatic sport, advisable for all ages and recommended to rehabilitate your body after suffering from a trauma or to lose weight without placing too much stress on your back and joints. Additionally, swimming strengthens your osteomuscolar system and improves both your respiratory and cardiocirculatory system (blood flows better to the extremities and your heart becomes stronger).

As in all resistance sports, swimming is a good way to burn calories; although, this happens only in specific conditions. First of all, you must swim for at least one hour; secondly you must swim continuously. This means that, during the sixty minutes you spend in the pool, you cannot spend most of your time sitting at the edge of the lane, watching others swim back and forth. It doesn't even work if you swim five laps of doggie paddle or thirty laps with long pauses to meditate in between. In order to get some benefits, you must swim for sixty minutes at medium speed, even allowing yourself proper time to rest between workouts.

When you are trained, you can burn between 200 and 600 calories, depending on the stroke and exercise you select. Swimming also contributes to tone your body thanks to the physical phenomenon known as "heat transfer." The temperature of a swimming pool, normally set between 26 and 28° degrees Celsius (78.8° - 82.4° Fahrenheit) is lower than that of a human being, so, in order to maintain balance, your body must intensify heat production, burning whatever is available (carbohydrates and fat). Compared to heat exchange in the air, this process occurs more quickly in water

(water is 25 times more efficient than air as a heat conductor) and is intensified by the continuous flow of fresh water over your skin (thermal convention). Thus swimming is a good way to regulate body weight; although, running and gym training produce visible results in less time. Another important peculiarity of this sport is that when you practice it, you are not just training your body, but also your mind. When you swim, you do so in an environment that is, in some way, primordial and isolated from the rest of the world, both visually and acoustically. In these conditions, your attention is captured by the stimuli sent by your body and mind, so it becomes so natural to listen and speak to yourself that you end up establishing a unique way to communicate with your inner self.

At the first stages of your aquatic experience, when you are still tackling floating issues or learning your strokes, in addition to dealing with your body's movements, your mind must face the attacks that, in an underhand manner, come from old auditory memories as scary phrases that you were told when you were a child, whose purpose was only to warn you from the dangers of water ("careful or you'll drown;" "if you get tired you won't make it back; "watch out for jellyfish;" "you will get congested"). Those innocent and caring gestures, which the adult said for your own good, can turn into a strong sense of discomfort or fear, now that you are an adult. You can overcome it only through brave mental work. You can leave it behind once and for all only by constantly training in the company of yourself.

If, to you, swimming means rolling through laps with the purpose of developing power and resistance, then your mind is essential to reach your performance objectives. Swimming is a strenuous sport that constantly puts your body under stress. As you move forward in your training, your body begins to tire and it becomes winy: it demands you slow down or stop and, sooner or later, it begins to beg for you to set aside all that pounding. Only your mind can keep it quiet. Only your mind can stubbornly return to the pool and find pleasure in that suffering for fatigue. Because you know it: your muscles burning, you feeling out of breath and your heart pounding in your chest are all signs that you are getting a good workout. So when you are exhausted, instead of feeling down, you are happy because you know that you set the bar a little higher and therefore increased your skills.

Swimming is the art of repeating movements and feelings. The effect of your movements drives slow and constant improvement in the water. It is almost a mathematical formula; the certain and foreseeable outcome gives you confidence. The only thing that can jeopardize this comfort zone is your coach requesting you to perform a correction. In these cases you may feel your balance waver. It is through the sole use of mental effort that you can succeed in returning to your swimming, inserting the new element and using it to your advantage. Only by putting your mind to it can you change the way your muscles contract, going from the old way of swimming to the newly desired way. One thing is for sure: when you reach your objective, you have proven to yourself that you can do anything.

Swimming is the most effective way to purify your spirit. Water flowing on your skin is like a caress that washes away stress and anxiety. The lack of gravity that keeps you suspended gives your body a liberating sense of lightness. The transparency before your eyes reflects clarity inside you, making you overcome any doubt.

When, at the end of the swim, you exit the pool, your body and mind feel a deep sense of peace. Sure, you are tired, but the sense of fulfillment generated by the endorphins makes you feel content and ready for the rest you deserve. It is easy to get used to all this. In fact, it is so easy that once it has become part of your life, you cannot live without it.

EMOTION
Those of us who swim on our lunch hour

"They recorded all the meets of the Melbourne World Cup and they stay up to watch them, just like you (and often next to you). They rejoiced watching Magnini's endeavors and Marin's bronze medal, while trying not to wake up the family. They analyzed Phelps' apneas, attempting them mentally right before going to sleep. You don't know who they are, but, if you look closely, you will recognize them because their eyes look like those of a panda bear. Even at the office, back in shirt and tie, their hair is still a little wet and they still have goggles marks around their eyes.

They are the lunchbreak swimmers. They went to swim lessons when they were children and they quit right before they could learn the flip turns and the dolphin kick. Now they have gone back to swimming, usually because of a friend (and their waistline). As opposed to the joggers, they don't speak much about their sport. If it weren't for their ridiculous marks on their faces, you probably would never know they swim. Those goggles, always those goggles, it will be months, maybe years before they learn to put them on correctly. Some are still safely using diving masks, resulting in an even larger circumference of the ring on their face. Not too long ago, I joined them too, adopting the ring around my eyes. In the past, they looked like desperate people who jumped on their scooter to go lock themselves up at the pool during the hour that they could otherwise use to breathe easily, chat outdoors and eat a plate of tortelli. Then, over time, I understood. An hour of lap swim, besides providing physical wellness, generates a semi-opiate state. The pool lifts your body weight and nullifies gravity by acting on that weight you feel on your shoulders and that brings you down as you walk on dry land. The soundproofing effect of the water and its gel-like, almost amniotic consistency favors a sort of regression to prenatal life, allowing you to be yourself and, at the same time, to be the free floating spirit looking in from outside that enormous blue tummy. This ability to split into two facilitates introspection. In my case, for example, it had been a while since I had spoken with myself with as much frankness and lucidity; it took the act of immersing myself and chasing the bubbles made by the feet of the guy in front of me as if they were the red lights of the car ahead while driving on foggy days. Having previously practiced jogging, and being familiar with the sound of my breathing and shoes pounding on the gravel at Villa Ada, it seemed impossible that one could manage to think without the aid of the gentle breeze of the pine trees and the dark patches they project toward the sky. Undoubtedly, one can, you bet. When you are alone under water, your thoughts find their way to where they belong, even the most daring visions, maybe precisely thanks to the abstractive 2x2 tile and the blue lines at the bottom of the lane. Now I understand the silence of swimmers in the locker room, a silence attributable to chess players and cosmonauts. They seem rested when they return to the office after swimming one hundred laps. Their skin will smell like chlorine for the rest of the day, but they won't care. They will be teased by their co-workers for those rings around their eyes, but they won't pay attention. You can provoke them in any way, but they will only answer with that seraphic smile of those who have just filled up on endorphins. They will even help you if you cannot finish your work in time. Just avoid asking them to come play five-a-side soccer on Saturdays afternoons; that's the only thing that infuriates them".

(From the front page of Gazzetta dello Sport, April 3, 2007)

EXERCISE

List the five reasons why you could begin to swim or, if you already swim, the five reasons why you swim.
1.
2.
3.
4.
5.

List the five challenges that have kept you from starting or, if you already swim, that you must face in order to swim.
1.
2.
3.
4.
5.

Now make an effort to find five reasonable and feasible solutions for the five obstacles that you listed above.
1.
2.
3.
4.
5.

This exercise is aimed at rationalizing problems and solving them, leveraging personal motivations for which swimming could be a good thing. Try to spend at least 10 minutes on this exercise.

CHAPTER 2: LESSON ONE

EXPERIENCE - It's all getting started

"I must get moving, I must get some exercise, I must sign up for swim lessons... and I must do it now!" After my important conversation with the doctor, mentally I couldn't help but whisper to myself words of support and urgency for the need to begin practicing a sport as soon as possible. I was anxious but determined to find a swimming pool where I could register for lessons, thinking over the details that could keep me from regaining my health. Then, selecting the facility became the most complicated thing in the world because it must be conveniently located and offer "excuse-proof" class times. I was so convinced that this issue was so important that I worked out every detail ahead of time so to not leave room for any sort of mental alibi.

I asked my friends, talked with relatives and called on acquaintances. I found out that Milan has several swimming pools, many of which are run by the city; therefore, they offer reasonable rates and comply with health code regulations. I was afraid to possibly catch a strange illness or a rare type of skin fungus, like I had done about ten years earlier at a gym. In the end I found the perfect swimming pool for me: located half way between my house and work, a fifteen-minute ride from both locations and offering beginners' courses from seven to eight in the evenings. I especially appreciated the course duration of only two months (June and July), which psychologically helped me overcome my initial hesitation and the strange idea that I could suddenly wake up and remember that I don't love to swim.

On the first day of swim lessons I found out that, in addition to being the shortest, summer courses are also the least crowded. Maybe it is because everyone is at the beach, or maybe everyone is already in perfect shape; all I know is that there were no more than a dozen people doing their warm-up exercises. We were told that doing "dryland" training before entering the water is very important because that is how you prepare our muscles to perform better and protect your body from injury. That may be so; however, during those fifteen minutes it felt like I burned through all my energy. After a short barefoot run, they made us do three series of abs, squats, push-ups, stretching, arm stretches, neck rotations and you name it. I felt hot, sweaty and already very tired. Acting cute, I told the instructor that I was satisfied and that I was ready to go home, as I didn't need any more exercising for one day. He laughed and then said, "You may go take a shower... then get in the water to swim laps!" I swallowed hard and wiped the smile off my face. It was my first day of swim lessons and something told me that I would not forget it easily.

After answering a few simple questions by the instructors ("how many laps can you swim?", "which strokes do you know?", "how long have you been swimming?"), I was told that the absolute beginner lane is the one that runs alongside the edge of the pool; the one that can be exited easily, if necessary. I was introduced to the ladies who shared the lane with me: a new mom who was a bit older than me, and the other one was an especially cheerful elderly lady. Our instructor was a tall and thin blond, who wore her hair up in a long pony tail and who had a strict and impatient look about her. So my time, my moment of truth and my ultimate test had finally arrived. I couldn't turn back anymore. I gathered my courage and entered the pool slowly, going down the steps and immersing myself in water to begin my first swim lesson as an adult...

What a strange feeling. I felt like a chick looking at his mom. The two ladies and I were in the water with our noses pointed up to look at the instructor; standing on high ground, the instructor seemed to have strange power over us. In fact, she did not hesitate to use her power as she asked us to swim "a couple of laps right away" to show her what we could do. Resorting back to my jokes, I asked the instructor if swimming for a few meters would be enough, but, oddly, she did not smile. To take time, I agreed with the ladies that I would go last. Inevitably, after they began swimming, it was my turn. I breathed in and took courage; I pushed off the wall to gain some meters, then, very slowly and trying very hard to remember everything I knew about swimming (that is to say, nearly nothing), I began to swim. I began by swimming freestyle, keeping my head under water and raising my head to breathe once, then twice, and finally I just kept my head out of the water because the lack of oxygen became unbearable. After a few strokes I decided to switch to swimming the best way I know: doggy paddle. I realized that I was just half way through the first lap and already out of it: out of breath, energy and swim strokes. But just when I thought that I had nothing else to show, I remembered the backstroke; so I lay on my back and began to inhale water, triggering a panic attack. I flipped over, grabbed the lane divider and somehow I completed my first lap. My fellow swimmers were already on their second lap. At this time my instructor said, in an exasperated and stern tone, typical of those people who want to make you feel even worse for being inept, (as in "let's humiliate him all the way,") "It's getting late!" I waited a few more seconds and then began swimming again. This time I had no strategy for my choice of swimming strokes. My arms and legs rotated at random, anything goes. I stopped at least two or three times, helping myself move forward by hanging on to the lane divider, as in "tug-of-war." When I reached the end of the lane, under the gaze of the instructor's long and obscure figure, I was completely worn-out. I was breathing hard, my eyes looked like they were falling out of their sockets and I felt an agonizing feeling of discomfort. After a moment of silence, the instructor said to us, with a smirk looking half way between sadistic and amused, "You can all float, some better than others...". Then, looking at me, she added, "Some much worse, to tell the truth... so although you can float, we must start from scratch with your technique. Grab a kickboard and let's begin with the first exercise." Begin? What do you mean begin!?! I think I am done for today! But how do I tell her? How do I let her know I am done without seeming disrespectful or rude? Let's see, I guess I could just say nothing at all...

Without noticing my facial expressions, through which anyone could have deciphered my unspeakable panic, she went on to explain what she expected from us: "Hold the kickboard by the handles and swim only with your feet: raise your head to breathe, then place your head under water and blow bubbles in the water. Two laps, go!" In my mind, one thing is for certain: I will never complete this exercise. And I am not wrong.

After finishing one exhausting lap, which took what felt

like an eternity, and after giving myself a break that lasted several minutes by using creative excuses such as, "my bathing suit came untied, there is water in my goggles" and "my shoulder bones are itching," I began to swim back. I swam for just a few meters and, at this point, my fear turned into a sad reality. My head started spinning, my body turned limp and I had the distinct feeling that I was on the verge of passing out. I used the last bit of energy left in me to pull myself out of the water and crawl onto the edge of the pool; I lay down on my side, looking like a whale stranded on a beach. At this point I finally caught the attention of my instructor, who decided to quit laughing with the lifeguard and come to my rescue. With their help, I pulled my face off the floor and they helped me reach the infirmary by supporting my weight. They laid me down on a stretcher, raised my legs and placed a blanket over me. They said that I looked pale, but not to worry because things like that happen sometimes.

I mentally reflected on a bizarre thought: could these be the most embarrassing 15 minutes of my life? My thoughts were interrupted by a good cup of warm tea with lots of sugar. I began to feel better and to over speak, inventing excuses and lies: "Well, I am just out of breath... darn it... at least I am in shape!" And my instructor said, "Right... quite in shape! But at your age, your lungs should be this big!" She used her hands to picture some imaginary specs larger than her own shoulders.

Not bad for my first swim lesson! The toughest moment came later, when, alone, weak and with my morale hanging lower than my rubber flip-flops, I went back to the locker room to take a shower.

That pattern did not change during the following lessons. During dryland training, I was worn out by warm-up exercises and then, once in the pool, instead of relaxing and floating, I got in a big fight with the water, which, in a matter of minutes, took away all my strength and led me closer and closer to another very humiliating fainting episode.

What hurt the most was realizing that commitment, efforts and, more generally, my will to keep trying were not rewarded at all; in fact, my pitiful results were always met by the ever more incredulous and disappointed looks of my instructor. It was plain to see in her eyes that I kept scoring more and more loser points. She was convinced to be witnessing quite a unique phenomenon: a young 27-year-old man, who was as worn-out and weak as an eighty-year-old retiree who had never practiced any sports in his life. On the other hand, I was convinced that completing two laps without stopping to catch your breath was an unattainable goal for an average human being. For this reason, I was suspicious of those individuals training in the lap swim lane that, judging by appearance, seemed to require no breaks as they swam back and forth.

When I returned to my senses after some sort of auto-hypnosis, I felt discouraged and I began to think that maybe there was something wrong with me, perhaps my body was built with a manufacturing defect, or that my legs were just too heavy to float. In just a few steps, my conclusion became the false belief that I was not cut out for this sport. As if that weren't enough, I felt extreme anxiety when I had to put my head under water and blow out air. I found it ridiculous, unnatural and it made my head spin. If I only knew that, as beginners, the world's greatest swimmers had lived through difficult moments like mine, maybe my situation would not have seemed so troublesome…

Ian and Michael are three years apart. Ian, the older of

the two, is Australian, while Michael is American. They were still children when they were first exposed to swimming and for both children the most difficult thing was to keep their head under water.

Ian was allergic to chlorine, a problem that forced him to alternate two weeks of training with one week of being out sick, during which he was treated with so many antibiotics that, to him, it all soon became a big joke. Nose clips alleviated the allergy, but during his first swim meet, Ian took them off and threw them away because he did not want to look different from other kids. His allergy tormented him for the best part of his childhood; nevertheless his parents continued to support him in practicing this sport that, as his instructors say, came to him as natural as walking.

Michael's story is different. His difficulty in placing his head under water was due to the simple fact that he did not even want to think about doing such a thing, so during the first few years in swimming he agreed to stay in the water only if he could keep his belly up. For a good part of his first swim course, which began at the age of seven, Michael only swam the backstroke, unlike other children who put their faces in the water and performed the tasks requested by their instructor. Michael cried constantly; he complained and threw temper tantrums. He did so to attract attention, also because during that time his father moved out of their home and gradually walked out of Michael's life. Two years later Michael was diagnosed with attention deficit disorder and hyperactivity: he had so much energy in his body that swimming became the vehicle through which he unloaded energy and controlled himself more than any other sport.

The rest is swim history. Ian Thorpe and Michael Phelps left an indelible mark in the World of swimming, taking home an impressive number of wins and medals. They did so after growing up cheering for their older sisters, who, although very talented, stopped competing before reaching the Olympics (Ian's sister quit due to strong difficulties in managing stressful moments, while Michael's sister had physical problems).

ANALYSYS - The lifeline

After my first swim lesson, I spent hours thinking of those moments as if I were the victim of a curse. Going over every scene made me feel pain and discouragement, but through it all I couldn't help but relive those moments. It was a need that seemed absurd and masochistic but today, after doing some research, I understand it more thoroughly.

When an important and exciting experience takes place in your life, whether good or bad, you may relive it in your mind hours later. It is something that happens automatically, and this allows you to relive the emotions of those moments. When those emotions are positive, the pleasure of reliving them triggers mental projection; when your emotions are negative, your desire to delete or diminish them drives the process. To better explain this mechanism, think of an experience as if it were a photograph. When you take a nice picture, you look at it again and again because it feels good. When the picture is ugly, you look at it over and over again to understand what's wrong with it. In your mind, projecting an ugly photograph may subconsciously push you to touch it up, diminishing or deleting the wrong details in order to make that memory more tolerable. This means that what you

37

experienced is often different from what you remember.

Reliving my first swim lesson, a loser's moment in my life, caused suffering. My brain re-proposed it because, before filing it away, it needed to spin it in a positive way so it could consider it "acceptable" with my objective to regain my health: I needed to perceive it as a step forward rather than a failure. This is the reason why, to me, that experience has become "my first swim lesson" (as in the beginning of my climb) and not "my first and last swim lesson" (the confirmation that by now my health was lost forever). But how did my brain succeed in giving a positive spin to a negative experience? It did so by simply mentally leveraging on the most painful episode of that time, an episode which, no matter the cost, must absolutely not be repeated again in my life...

It was a Saturday afternoon, just a regular Saturday afternoon. I went into this clothing store because I needed a new pair of trousers. Lately it was something that I did often because my trousers kept getting tighter and tighter, and they became uncomfortable to wear. Over the last three years, my sedentary life as an employee had provided me with stable income and accumulated adipose tissue around my waistline, which forced me to constantly renew my wardrobe. Oh well, your body type can change over time; as my mother said, I was becoming a man. Anyway, I would like to point out that I didn't have a belly, like Bud Spencer's, my father's and my uncle's, although the previous summer my cousin had said something that had made me stop and think.

We had met a guy on the beach who played volleyball with us. I remember that this guy was as tall as me, about the same age as me and he had a lean physique with visibly developed muscles as I always had, too, so it came natural for me to say: "Well, he's more or less like me, right?" With similar candor, my cousin had replied, "You are joking, right?" No, I wasn't joking, but I still hadn't realized my slow transformation.

Ah, here was a nice pair of trousers! I really wanted to try those on. The trousers were my size, a 38. I never understood why, since I had grown into this size, my trousers had become super long. Something must have changed in the textile industry because I remembered that, in the past, when I had bought trousers, they had fit me perfectly, both in the waist and length. I folded up these trousers to see how they would hang once they were hemmed up, but I pulled up my zipper first. I lifted my shirt and I looked into the mirror to see how I looked. They were almost too tight. Feeling a little sad, I told myself, "I may have to move up to a 40." I bent over to fold up my pants one more time, when, all of a sudden, I felt out of breath. I stood up quickly, I unbuttoned my trousers, and I could finally relax my abdomen.

Without even noticing, I had been unconsciously holding my breath so that I could fit in those trousers. I stood in front of the mirror and I carefully looked at my reflection: the neon light was bright and it made me look like a ghost wearing unbuttoned trousers. I turned, looked at my profile and noticed, for the first time, that my belly was soft and extending way beyond my pecs line. No doubt, I had quite a belly! I felt like I was going to pass out, my stomach tightened and my eyes fogged up a little. It lasted only for a moment, and I physically quickly bounced back, but mentally I remained in front of that mirror for weeks, looking at that image of myself, turned to one side, trying to button up a pair of trousers that had no intention of containing me.

When I was done torturing myself through this mental

process, I experienced a strange feeling. It happened one morning, when I was in front of the mirror at home. I carefully looked at my face; then, in a natural way, I looked myself straight in the eye and I slowly and decisively told myself: "That's it!"

Having a little belly, in itself, is no source of suffering. If I didn't have one, my problems would be quite different. It does not pain me either, within certain limits, to have a belly. That's not the point. In this episode of my life, what caused negative sensations is the fact that I broke my own personal physical health rules, and that I did so without even realizing what I was doing. It is a little like you being against smoking because you feel like it is bad for you; then you begin to smoke three cigarettes a day because you think that true addiction is something else until you have to come to grips with reality when you start experiencing an insistent morning cough.

To me, respecting the rule of having a "limited belly," together with many others, such as, for example, "not being out of breath after five steps" or "not catching the flu more than once a season" means satisfying one of my cornerstone values: my health. I feel healthy, therefore I am happy; otherwise I feel pain. What tells me whether I am leaning more to one side rather than the other are my rules, which make me feel good, otherwise I feel bad. The mechanism of values and rules works for me as well as for you; although, we rarely realize how much such mechanisms affect our daily humor.

When I reached the state of mind of a person who realizes that he has broken one of his rules and decides to take a step back no matter what, I felt a bit like I had given myself a very powerful armor to resist any other type of pain, such as fatigue, sense of incapacity or inadequacy, physical discomfort and derision by the lifeguards. Nothing could have stopped me from going back and regaining my health: when facing every swimming challenge, every difficulty and every suffering, all I had to do is recall that image of myself in the mirror of that clothing store to remind me of that discomfort that I would never want to experience again in my life.

Scientifically speaking, by linking a state of mind (the discomfort) with a stimulus (the image in the mirror) that could easily be activated by me, I created my lifeline. All it took was recalling that memory that, within me, triggered the order, "run away and get as far as you can from that most negative experience." My lifeline, just as the anchor on a boat, allowed me to stay grounded.

As you can see, this is a very powerful mechanism that leads to great results and, sometimes, it may also lead to major failures. With a little focus and research you can develop great control over your mental state, so much so that you can learn to put yourself in the right conditions to produce the results you desire.

As you read on, you will learn what I was able to achieve when I learned to use this technique in a conscious way; meanwhile, I would like to tell you how an American boy named Mark reached exceptional results by implementing a plan similar to mine since he was a child...

As opposed to his American peers, who had fun playing basketball, football or baseball, Mark loved to swim. As opposed to many of Mark's friends' parents, who were light years away while their children were in sports, Mark's father participated in and encouraged Mark's endeavors. Mark's father, Arnold was very affected by the loss of his

father at an early age. He was just seven years old. What hurt Arnold deeply was that on the day his father was brought to the hospital, Arnold had built a bridge over a canal and he wanted his father to see it at all costs. Then, Arnold's father's condition worsened and, although he had promised to go see his son's work, he died. The pain of not having had his father by his side left an indelible mark in Arnold's childhood, so he promised himself that he would always be there for his children.

Now that he was a father, Arnold constantly participated in Mark's life, and he did not hesitate to use harsh and strict methods to help his son reach his goals. The most common phrases with which he psychologically conditioned his son included: "Swimming is not everything, winning is: "How many out of the eight lanes win the meet? One, and only one, keep that in mind!" Over time, it was inevitable for Mark to always expect the best from himself, which led him to see winning as the only acceptable outcome, as well as to become a bragger.

At age nine, Mark attended his first swim meet at the swimming pool. His previous swimming experience consisted of swimming in the waves of the ocean and some pool training. That was all, besides a short explanation of what to do during the meet: "Dive in, swim one lap and touch the wall." He did exactly as he was told, so he dove in, swam as fast as lightning and arrived first in his heat. As a prize, Mark received a nice purple ribbon, of which he was especially proud for a few minutes, as he was convinced to be the only swimmer to have been given one. At the end of the swim meet, Mark realized that three other boys received respectively a blue ribbon for first place, a red ribbon for second place and a white ribbon for third place, so he demanded an explanation. They told him that those three children's racing times were not only the best in their individual heats, but also of all those who had raced that day. No longer feeling best, Mark grabbed his ribbon, threw it on the ground and said with disgust, "I hate purple ribbons... I hate white ribbons and red ribbons, too! I only want to win blue ribbons!"

Mark kept his word. He began to swim brilliantly and more quickly until the time when, a few years later, swimming in the 17-18-year-old category, he won an impressive series of victories and records. At the age of 17, he won five gold medals at the Pan-American Games, effectively becoming an international champion.

For eighteen-year-old Mark Spitz, 1968 was a revealing year in his sports career because he had to prove his worth at the Olympic Games in Mexico City. Mark boasted with confidence; he was sure he was the best and he could conquer an incredible goal of five gold medals. However, by the end of the Olympics, he was disappointed to go home with only two gold medals, and they were just for relay races. In individual events (100 and 200-meter butterfly, as well as 100-meter freestyle) he "only" won one bronze and one silver medal. For Mark, this was a bitter defeat, which pained him tremendously, and this situation was made even more unbearable by a voice in his head that continued to say, "Swimming is not everything, winning is!"

Although he was down, defeated and in a state that he considered unacceptable, Mark didn't quit; in fact, he devoted all his energy to swim training, convinced that he could exceed his limits.

Four years later, Mark tried it again and he won big at the Munich Olympics. He was more cautious, concentrated, mature and determined. He took on every single event as if it were a final. The news from those days described him as "a Martian," not only because he won four individual gold medals and additional medals in the relays, setting the record for individual medals in a single edition of the Olympic Games, but also because he did so by establishing seven world records.

At the early age of twenty-two and after participating in the Olympics that made him memorable in the world's history of swimming, Mark Spitz retired with a very simple explanation: "I could not do better. I feel like the guy who built the perfect machine".

EMOTION
The force within

Try to think of it for a moment and you will see it come to you.

Try to think about it and even you will perfectly remember a time when you felt capable of everything. That time you thought that nothing could stop you, that you had everything you needed, and that you could quickly obtain anything you wished for.

Try to think about it, because everyone at least once in their life feels invincible. Maybe it was a just period you went through or maybe it lasted for some time. Maybe it happened when you received your first paycheck or when, at school, instead of the usual C, you earned a B or, better yet, an A. Maybe it happened when you succeeded in kissing someone for the first time. Or maybe it was when you finally earned your diploma or degree. It could have been that time when you had your first job, that time when you scored a goal, won a swim event, or performed well at a dance recital.

Try to think about it and relive those moments for a few seconds. Close your eyes. Relax.

Think of those moments. Recall those images, words and feelings. Recreate that atmosphere. Remember the detail, focus on the faces and settings that surrounded you. Try to smell the scents, listen to the noises and sounds. Recreate that moment as if it were now and here; listen to your heart beating differently and your breathing differently as your body assumes an unexpectedly confident stance.

Take notice: now that your mind has returned to such an important, gratifying and exciting moment, your soul is reliving life moments during which everything appeared easy and possible; you will then notice that your body has also gone back to that moment: your head is turned the same way and that your shoulders, back and legs are also positioned the same way as they were at that time. Your body has resumed the same position as then.

After you experience this, open your eyes.

Now that you feel it, you are ready to face a new challenge with the same spirit and winning energy that have brought you joy once before.

EXERCISE

Next to each bullet, write an element that represents happiness or makes you happy.

-
-
-
-
-
-
-

For each of the items listed above, identify and describe limits, or things that, if they happened, would make you feel unhappy.

-
-
-
-
-
-
-

Now take some time to reflect on each single element, asking yourself if, in this phase of your life, you find yourself below or above those standards you have identified.

CHAPTER 3: I CAN

EXPERIENCE - From ten to thirty-six laps

So, through bad impressions and awkward attempts, I completed my first swimming course for adults. The only thing I managed to improve during those two months was my ability to digest chlorine; as for the rest, I received extremely hard lessons on the fact that, in order to advance in the art of swimming, one needs great amounts of patience and perseverance. I received proof of this in August, on a scorching hot summer day, when I felt the uncontrollable desire to jump in the water...

I was with some friends, soaking in the waters of an enclosed swimming pool in Milan, and it was of no consequence that the ceiling kept us from getting a suntan and seeing the clouds in the sky; we just wanted a break from the unpleasant sticky feeling and exhausting breathing challenge caused by the heat. Feeling refreshed and renewed by splashing in fresh water, my friends and I came up with the idea that we could exercise while remaining in the water. All caught up in the moment, I made one of the most compromising statements of my life: "Alright guys, now I will demonstrate how to swim! I am taking a course!" My foolishness gave me strength, so I swam two laps without stopping. All of a sudden I realized that I was out of breath and energy, so I began feeling like an animal shot with a tranquilizer. After completing lap four, which I took on after a few moments of rest, I decided to give a demonstration of the event that gave me celebrity status a few weeks earlier: passing out in public.

Having extensive experience in this field, I felt it coming on while my senses were going out so, without hesitation, I sprinted out of the water like a cat and I quickly headed towards my towel. As I lay down, I was still partially conscious; next, I fell down so loudly that it must have scared the birds away from the trees. With nonchalance I raised my legs and positioned the heels of my feet on a backpack, reaching the classic stance of somebody who is feeling ill. I held that position without muttering one word for about ten minutes, as my friends joked and made fun of me. A strange thought lurked inside me: "Is this what I deserve for not having practiced sports for such a long time?"

Upon my return from summer vacation, I was motivated, determined; I highly desired to move forward in my aquatic adventure. I went to the pool and, without hesitation I proceeded to sign up for the winter swim course for adults. First, however, I had to deal with an endless line of mothers waiting to enroll their children in the courses reserved for them. Judging by the crowds, I suspected that the pool gets busy in the winter, unlike the summer, when the facility is semi-deserted.

My suspicion was quickly confirmed. On the first day of class, there were so many of us warming up that they made us run around in a circle, single file and one way. As we went on with our exercises, personal space was limited and, at every movement, we ran the risk of clamorously slapping our neighbor.

The age of the participants varied. There were two ladies in their fifties that complained of back pain, young mothers that couldn't wait to lose the extra pounds gained during pregnancy and kids over sixteen talking about school tests and oral presentations. By taking a closer look, I noticed that the most populous age group was 30 to 40, which typically is that age in which women and men begin to acknowledge the fact that they are no longer kids and that, due to metabolism changes, their stomachs have grown larger creating extra curves of varying thickness and consistency.

As we completed our warm-up exercises, similarly to what happens on the first day of school when teachers call out their classes, our swim instructors called attendance and placed us in various levels: the least aquatically inclined went to Beginners 0; those who could barely float went to Beginners 1, intermediate swimmers went to Intermediate and swim prodigies went to Advanced. Each level was assigned one lane and each lane was supervised by an instructor. I surprisingly received a field promotion from level 0, which I had attended in the summer, to Beginners 1. I asked myself if this was a joke, given the fact that you are assigned a group based on your initial responses (they asked, "Which strokes do you know? How many laps can you swim?" and I replied, "A little freestyle and a little backstroke, for a few seconds"). My responses were exactly the same as when I signed up for the previous course. Then, as I looked over at those who were in my old lane, I figured out what had changed: in the winter, the Beginners 0 group is reserved for those who need to learn to tread water, that is to say that they swim by grabbing the edge of the pool or by desperately holding on to a floating device.

The instructor who called my name was a robust young

man with serious and commanding mannerism and who, in addition to being in an incredible hurry ("get these laps done quickly, they are waiting for me at home tonight!"), was a lover of activities that involve throwing objects, meaning that he did not hesitate to fling arm floats or kickboards at those who dared not comply with his orders. His human targets, which moved along the surface of the water, included me, a couple of teenagers, a grandpa and his granddaughter, some university students and some other individuals of indecipherable age. There were approximately ten of us swimming: too many for a single lane and a crowd considering that, generally speaking, our swim abilities were limited and that the only thing that we knew how to do well was flounder as cods making high waves for those who, just like me, couldn't help but swallow water. Just when I thought that I had enough to drink, being a little drunk on chlorine and a little worried about my health, I asked the instructor: "Question: if I drink too much chlorine, what is the worst thing that can happen to me?" He very nicely answered, "You will pay for it at the other end!"

A second inconvenience caused by crowding was fender-benders. Sometimes I was the one who ran into the swimmer ahead of me, and other times, especially when swimming backstroke kick only, my fellow swimmers ran into me, causing me to sink.

To cap it all, in order to listen to the instructor, who was strategically standing by the deep end of the lane, where your feet touch the bottom only if you are 6 foot five, we battled for a spot to hold on to the edge of the pool so we could rest without having to work so hard to stay afloat. The question that we were all asking ourselves was: if the lane has two ends, and only one of these is at the deep end, why do instructors choose to position themselves there as it is so inconvenient for us? It is obvious that, as we were having trouble staying afloat, we ended up grasping anything that helped, such as lane dividers, and obviously the instructor scolded us by 'nicely' saying: "...you're going to break that! How many times do I have to tell you that you are not perched up chickens?"

If all this weren't enough, I must deal with my chronic weakness, a small but growing discomfort that, at the end of every swim, made me feel lightheaded. Exactly because I am an incurable optimist, I tried to investigate the matter by turning to the instructor, who surprised me once more by giving me an answer full of practical implications: "It's called hyperventilation: you must blow out all the air you breathe in, otherwise your brain begins floating in oxygen. So, before you breathe in, be sure to blow out all the air you already have in your lungs. Get it, Mr. Enzo Maiorca?" I did exactly as I was told, blowing out the air under water and making lots of bubbles. For a moment, I thought that this way I could make a whirlpool and get some money doing it; then, when I was out of breath, I realized that, at the most, I could get some pats on the back for blowing up one or two balloons at a children's party. The only remedy that seemed to have any effect against my sense of weakness was a spoonful of honey, which I avidly swallowed before getting in the water. To make sure that I truly tried everything, I asked my fellow course members if they experienced the same thing, but apparently I was the only one. Someone timidly suggested watching my diet, so I thought about what I ate by visualizing the complete menu from the bar by the office, and I concluded that my diet could certainly not be my problem. Oh gosh, maybe it's because I skipped my snack! Precisely because I have a slow digestive system, on the days that I went to the pool I avoided eating in the afternoons.

This meant that I was forcing my stomach to fast for seven hours before physical activity. Could this be my problem?

From a technical viewpoint, the goal of Beginners 1 was to improve our freestyle and backstroke. For this reason, our lessons centered on tiring and boring exercises that called for us to swim laps using only one arm or just kicking our feet.

In the middle of the season, they gave us a new objective: learn the basics of breaststroke. As long as all we had to do was put into practice some corrections for a stroke I already knew, then I can say that I successfully achieved something; however, when the goal at hand was to perform new movements whose knowledge was to be acquired from our instructor demonstrating what we should be doing in the water by ridiculously lying down at the edge of the pool the situation just got more complicated, the greatest difficulty consisted in turning those strange arm and leg movements into advancing in water. I did exactly what the instructor had demonstrated: drawing a circle with my hands and a triangle with my feet and, just like him, my result was total statics! Of course, total statics is fully natural for him as he was demonstrating out of the water, but I was not at all convinced that by performing those movements in the water one could advance in any direction.

Quantitatively speaking, half way through the swim season I calculated that, over thirty minutes, I could swim sixteen laps, rounding up. Not bad if you think of when I was just starting out, but very depressing if I compared myself to others who swam regularly. One day, after listening to me telling all about my progress, a co-worker of mine, who is approximately sixty years old, candidly revealed: "So true, I also enjoy swimming. I too swim my 20-30 laps twice a week, easily. I agree: your health is the most important thing." That small humiliation that I felt when hearing such statements gave me incredible motivation. I kept telling myself: "...if she can do it, and she is no athlete and twice my age, then I can do it, too!"

Toward the end of the swim season I realized that I had lost weight and that I felt decisively better. I was no longer tight and buffed as when I was younger, but for the first time in years I realized that I had halted what seemed to be an inescapable process of physical dilation and succeeded in reversing its effects. If I could only change my horrible eating habits, the beneficial effects would be even more evident; conversely for the moment I continued to neutralize all my efforts at the pool by overeating unhealthy foods.

With the beginning of the summer course, I was officially into my second year of swimming. As expected, the number of participants dropped dramatically, but, instead of being upset about it, this time I looked at the positive side: with less people, instructors would be able to pay more attention to us than they did during the winter course. So, thanks to the nice weather and the ever decreasing hits by leg floats, during the last few lessons I realized that I had reached three very important goals: firstly, I could swim thirty-six laps in approximately one-half hour; secondly, even my breaststroke, although lopsided, was finally moving forward; thirdly, my swallowing pool water had decreased to just couple of times during my lessons. I received positive proof of my progress, not unusually, on a sunny day in July...

When, as an Italian, I chose to go on vacation to a hotel popular with Italians, I knew that all Italians almost inevitably end up getting to know each other within a couple of days of arriving. Social relations are made easier and more pleasant by the relaxed setting and by the custom of saying hello even to people you don't know. Without

even realizing it, you find yourself talking with people whom you would have never even noticed, and this tells you that sometimes appearances are deceiving but, almost always, they are exactly right. Small talk, a little swimming and, sooner or later, familiarity sets in. One afternoon, as all afternoons during this vacation, I was about to jump in the swimming pool of the hotel for my daily swim. I told myself to swim at least twenty laps a day: ten for not forgetting my strokes and ten for staying fit. I wanted to dive in without hesitation, but I felt almost hypnotized by the water, which appeared very cold next to my skin warmed up by the sun; I couldn't help but think of the thermal shock that would result from jumping in the water. I kept thinking of what I should do when, all of a sudden, someone behind me grabbed me and pushed me in the pool. In a fraction of a second I realized that this was the usual prank, so, partly for revenge and a partly for play, I quickly stretched out my hand, grabbed and dragged into the water the jester behind me. I swam to the surface, grinned and looked around to identify the person responsible for the joke: as it turns out... it was the girl from the umbrella next to mine! To continue the game, I grabbed her knees with my feet and, thrusting my back, I pulled her under water, enjoying the results of my actions. Then I realized that she was taking a bit too long to re-emerge. I was a bit puzzled, also because the water was only a couple of meters deep. When she finally reappeared, reality turned into what looked like a movie in slow-motion and I saw that her face had the typical expression of terror of those who desperately try to yell something like: "Help, I am drowning!" Realizing what was happening, I dove in after her. She grabbed my neck and began to squeeze, making me feel like a chicken during its last moments of life. I tried to break free, but no luck. I decided to swim as quickly as possible to the edge of the pool. I moved my legs as quickly as I could; then, with one, two, three strokes I grabbed the edge of the pool and saved the unfortunate woman, who was just about ready to kill me. I was worn-out and the scare made my eyes feel like they were falling out of their sockets; a little speechless, I asked: "You... you don't know how to swim?" She replied, laughing: "Ah-ah... no! But that was so much fun!"

Although I was just a beginner with a very limited technique and a ridiculous amount of breath, I performed a successful rescue à la Baywatch. Would I be cast for the thirteenth season of the television series?

ANALYSIS - It's a matter of method

You too may have realized that when you want to learn a new physical or recreational skill, the method most widely used is imitation: the teacher performs the movement; you look at the movement, memorize it and try to repeat it as closely as possible. This can be said for dancing, martial arts, swimming, aerobics and many other sports. The advantage of using this system is that it allows instructors to manage multiple students learning at the same time; the disadvantage is that, by showing the technique only through visual stimuli, students must satisfy themselves with one third of the information necessary to learn correctly, as no teaching is imparted by touching or hearing, which would contribute to develop sensitivity and a sense of rhythm.

Good teachers are well aware of the drawbacks of a method only based on imitation, so they integrate their demonstrations with other types of stimuli, such as coming into contact with students to correct posture and movements or by marking rhythm by clapping hands, tapping feet or using their voice. It's a little like the karate instructor does when, walking down the rows of students standing in the defensive stance, he tries to push them in every direction to check their stability or hit them to test their resistance and reflexes. It's just like it was done by Master Miyagi with student Daniel San in the movie Karate Kid, when, after shaking his student a couple of times, Miyagi said: "Too soft you are! If I push, you rock; if I hit, you hard and steady!"

In non-competitive couple dances, the most skilled male dancers are those who look like extraordinary circus dancers as they are those who, while keeping the rhythm, know how to communicate their commands to their partners without saying a word. Vice-versa, good female dancers are those who adapt themselves to the male dancer, follow the males and interpret the offered possibilities while keeping up with the rhythm and avoiding creating opposition to the man's lead by attempting to anticipate him and impose themselves, distorting the rules of dancing. Even in swimming, sensitivity and rhythm play an important role in learning the technique. This is proven by modern swim courses for children, which more often than not require the instructor to spend time in the water with his students in order to play and swim with them, holding their tiny bodies while positioning them in the correct stance and shape tomorrow's good swimmers. This is also proven by courses for youngsters that move on to competitive swimming, who, in addition to training in the water, must attend sessions of dryland training that have nothing to do with aerobics or stretching. These sessions are based on exercises that improve sensitivity and rhythm. They normally require the athlete to lie down on a bench and simulate her strokes, while the instructor corrects the position of her hands and feet, stimulating muscle memory in the key points of the stroke (entry, pull, push and recovery). To explain what happens, I will explain in detail in order for you to possibly perform a similar exercise: imagine that you see an athlete lying down on a bench face down; now you see her mimic freestyle while she pretends to place her hand in the water over her head almost looking like she is placing a letter into a mailbox; at this point the instructor asks to hold that position in order to apply pressure on the palm of the athlete's hand; then the instructor applies pressure on the forearm, head and other parts of the body while the athlete holds the position generating the correct resistance. As the movement is repeated multiple times, the exercise helps memorize the points of the body where the swimmer must feel pressure as those are the indicators of a correct stroke layout.

If swim courses for young people are laid out in a way that allows individuals whose early developing bodies may easily learn the swim strokes, then what is the structure used in courses for adults, whose advanced age makes the learning process slower and more difficult? Well, as nobody expects to find talent in a swim course for adults, in most cases the teaching system used for older participants is only mimicking, supported by oral instructions, whose effectiveness varies according to the instructor's communication abilities.

Thus the framework is quite discouraging, as those adults who wish to learn to swim find themselves in the most unfavorable conditions: their bodies are not very flexible and the teaching methods reserved for them are even less structured. To give you an idea of how complicated it is to learn to swim as a grown up, I will give you some concrete examples. Let's begin from a simple but decisive factor: when you need to learn a gesture by imitating somebody, that somebody should be next to you and not elsewhere. It's an obvious, yet not trivial fact. The Karate instructor who is demonstrating how to strike usually stands next to you, and not in the next room. The dance instructor who teaches you a new dance step usually stands in front of you and not suspended above you; otherwise you wouldn't be able to see a thing and you would misunderstand what you need to do.

Conversely, the swim instructor does not enter the water and stand next to you, but rather she stands in her comfortable, dry spot and demonstrates vertically what you need to horizontally in the water. The worst part is that, although she flounders in the air, completing strokes that have no effect in terms of movement, you have to repeat those strokes in the water while trying to advance a few meters. What follows from that is always the same scenario: The instructor demonstrates the movement; you look at it very carefully and you memorize it; you are sure that you have completely understood how to do it; you get in the water and repeat exactly the same thing, but you notice that you don't move forward at all, regardless of your effort and commitment. At this point the instructor says: "It doesn't go like that, it goes like this, look here!" You look at the instructor, arching your eyebrows because you see the exact same thing that you saw before, as the human brain reasons within frameworks and therefore always focuses on the same details, so you do exactly what you did before, repeating the same mistakes. Then, considering that you are not the only participant in the course and that there are many others in the exact same situation as you, the instructor pays attention to you only every three to four laps, which is just enough time for your mind to forget what you learned before and force you to begin all over again. And so this process continues to infinity because the same instructions, words and visual demonstrations followed the same way always yield the same results.

Another thing stands true: most adults that sign up for a swim course don't have very high expectations because they are content to enjoy their lesson as a simple pastime after work. What they learn is more than enough to satisfy their appetite for learning and therefore the courses offered, on average, meet the participants' expectations. Then considering that swimming pool budgets are chronically in the red, it is inevitable that an instructor is assigned more people than he/she can handle without ever having the possibility to enter the water, except sporadically. The same goes for dryland exercises. My experience tells me that, after spending a day at work or on the books, the only thing you feel like doing when you get to the pool is jump in your lane and stretch a little in the water. Forget lying down on a bench and perform strange exercises!

At this point, you could ask yourself what a motivated beginner can do to improve his/her technique. Well, I cannot say the absolute best thing to do; however, I can tell you what I did to satisfy my desire to improve. It all began from a sentence that I repeated to myself a thousand times: "Don't ever be satisfied with what you are told and shown. Use those suggestions as starting points for your own personal journey. Try to experiment for yourself." I am never fully satisfied with what I am taught; that's why, in addition to beginner level swim lessons twice a week, I always tried to go to the swimming pool on Saturdays and Sundays to train by myself. During one of these days I become aware of a terrifying swimming defect...

It's fun to swim laps. You pay an entrance fee, put on your bathing suit, jump in wherever you like (usually lanes with women and the elderly are the best, avoiding those with children and fast swimmers) and you proceed to do whatever you like. You can do some freestyle, backstroke and doggy paddle; then you can stop to look at the others struggling to swim back and forth and, without having anyone tell you what to do, by the end of the hour you feel like you haven't worked hard at all. When you do all this

with a friend, who feels the same way as you do, it's twice the fun.

One day I experienced just that. It was Sunday morning and I was in the pool with a friend of mine, an engineer, and, after completing a few laps of breaststroke and backstroke, and not before having joked on the resistance of those who seem like they are never tired, we decided to try some freestyle. In a totally unforeseeable way, at one point we were side by side and we began racing each other. Barely four laps later (you see, we are great athletes!) we were forced to stop because we were out of breath and energy. In between breaths I looked at my friend and said, "Man, it's hard work to swim fast! After five meters we can't take it anymore!" And he said, "It's quite a mystery how you can swim so far, considering that you swim like a tractor trailing a plow!" I looked at him to understand to what extent his statement was just a joke; then out of curiosity I asked, "What do you mean?" He replied, "When you swim, your legs hang so low that you look like you are almost standing! Looking from one side, you look like you are not lying on top of the water, but at an angle, almost vertically! It is obvious that if you lay at that angle your body is dragging your legs, as if they were a trailer. Do you know what that means?" My answer is complete silence as I wait for him to continue explaining: "Imagine you find yourself on top of a moving train, just like we often see in action movies. A crazy thing to do, but I am just mentioning it as an example. In a similar situation what could be the best thing to do to avoid falling off the train: standing up or laying down?" My response: "Sorry, but what does that have to do with it?!" "It does. You see, moving in water is kind of like being on top of a moving train, facing a wall made of air rather than water. In both situations, in order to advance minimizing your effort, your best bet is to lie as horizontally as possible." Although some aspects of his example remained unclear, by listening to him I began feeling like wind was blowing over my entire body, an experience that somehow made me realize how important it is to keep as horizontal as possible. However, I was still puzzled and I said, "Listen, I may not swim in a perfectly horizontal position, but your saying that my legs hang down sounds a bit exaggerated. Don't you think that if that were the case I would have noticed?" With a strange smirk on his face, he said to me: "Let's try something: I will sit at the bottom of the lane, crisscross my legs as the bottom is not very deep and you can swim over me. There is a one-meter gap between my head and the surface of the water. If it is like you say, when you swim over me you won't even come close to touching me. I only have one request: please hurry because I can only hold my breath for up to twenty seconds, okay?" "Okay, don't worry; I will zoom by you!" He sat at the bottom of the lane and I began to swim. After a few strokes, I was 'hovering' over him. I went past him with my head, then my chest and then I approached him with my legs: much to my surprise, I began to furiously kick his head and this forced him to emerge quickly. I looked at him and sadly conceded, "I am a horrible swimmer! I am dragging my legs... so maybe I should just stand!"

My desire to learn quickly brought me to process a series of solutions, which have become strong convictions. For this reason I feel like I should suggest that, if you are attending a swimming course for beginners and you wish to improve quickly, in addition to attending your lessons and listening to your instructors, from time to time you could benefit from swimming on your own so to find yourself in a stress-free situation (no instructors, fellow swimmers, waves, etc.)

giving you the opportunity to attempt those exercises that you find most useful for you, even if you are moving at snail pace. Take all the time you need. If you could show your movements to another swimmer who is at your level, so that you can exchange information each other's strokes. In the end, the instructor always looks at you from above the lane and never from one side; therefore, you may find areas that need improvement. Play while you swim, have fun, make up the most funky exercises to develop your awareness and you'll improve in a jiffy.

Here's another suggestion. By chance, I have often changed swim instructors. Sometimes it happened because I moved up swim levels and other times it happened simply because the instructor changed jobs. I noticed that changing instructors, especially when you are a beginner, favors learning as it increases the variety of corrections and exercises while dramatically improving your probability of receiving instructions in words that are most appropriate for the way you communicate. Let me explain. Every instructor uses words, examples and explanations that come from his/her personality. You may have noticed that, when you have generic conversations with people, you immediately understand some people while others sound like they came from another planet. Well, if you continue training with the same instructor who speaks Martian, you improvement may be limited by this factor. If you change instructors, you will have better chances to find one who uses the language that is the most appropriate for you. One last piece of advice: visual impressions are most powerful, therefore when you are immersed in water try to use your curiosity to observe the others. By naturally observing others, you could pick up details that no instructor, as excellent as she may be, could ever tell you.

EMOTION
The most important discovery

There are people who face sports with extreme ease because they have been practicing them since they were children. Others, on the other hand, stumble upon such sports as adults: they catch the bug, they try to practice them, they make an effort, but they often feel like they don't have what it takes. For both classes of people, sooner or later these activities become challenges. For the former, the challenge consists of chasing excellence. For the latter, the challenge is acquiring the skill. For the former, what matters is getting ahead of their competitors. For the latter, it is fundamental to break through limits that consist of high walls made of worry, fear and negative beliefs accumulated throughout life.

The former become bright, expert and professional. The latter become strong and big men and women. Whether you fall under the first or second category, what matters is that you enjoy the ride, a ride filled with satisfaction, suffering and discoveries that help you grow, which everyone knows as "life."

EXERCISE

When somebody explains something to you, it may happen that you don't understand them right away. This does not happen because you are stupid or your counterpart is unable to explain herself, but simply because the communications channel that they use is different from the one you prefer. You may prefer **listening** to the details while she makes you experience them, or maybe you prefer **seeing them** while she allows you to listen to them, or maybe you prefer **trying them** while she just wants to shows them to you. To help isolate your preferred method of learning among hearing, seeing or touch, try to answer the following questions:

1. When somebody explains a new movement to me, in order to understand it better, I need to: (A) try it, (B) see it, (C) listen to instructions on how to perform it.
2. When somebody explains a mechanism to me (for example an online checking account), I need to: (A) try it, (B) see it/see a diagram, (C) listen to instructions and details.
3. When I talk of my vacations, I like to tell: (A) what I did, (B) what I saw, (C) what I learned – history, culture, etc.
4. In school I always preferred: (A) summarizing using notes, (B) underlining books, (C) listening to the teacher.
5. When I think of swimming: (A) my thoughts focus on my feeling of strain and contact with the water, (B) my thoughts focus on images of water, the pool or myself, (C) my thoughts focus on the sounds of water and my breathing.

If most of your answers are A, your preferred method of learning is to try things out. If most of your answers are B, your preferred method of learning is seeing things. If, on the other hand, you answered mostly C, your preferred method of learning is listening to instructions.

CHAPTER 4: FINE-TUNING

EXPERIENCE – Breaststroke to butterfly

The month of September had always given me the blues. When I was in school, September meant that it was time to go back indoors after spending almost three very active months outdoors. For as long as I have had a job, September had been the month during which I returned to my daily routine after spending two to three weeks relaxing and not doing much of anything. Now that I was swimming, September had become an electrifying month, not so much because I was not working (it's hard to quit), but rather because I turned my attention to a positive event that I looked forward to do: restarting organized sports. No doubt: I had now developed a passion for swimming. While talking and telling stories of how much fun it is to soak in the pool and swim laps, I sort of performed a miracle. My cousin, who is the laziest person on earth, was so impressed by my swimming stories and the physical and mental benefits of swimming that he decided to quit collecting dust and join me at the pool, provided that the facilities were in a convenient location. We are about the same age; although he is taller and stronger than me, in the water we shared the same speed and endurance. The difference lied in the fact that while I am more in shape, he is technically better equipped.

To make our arrangement work for both of us, we set out to find a swimming pool conveniently located half way between my house and his, and, just as expected, we wound up selecting the pool by his house. The facility was cute and the staff was nice; the only hang-up was that our swim course was held on Mondays and Wednesdays, instead of Monday through Thursday or Tuesday through Friday. I experienced an empty feeling as my weekdays were now filled with inactivity; I kept asking myself, "What will I do on those days when I am not swimming?" Will I forget all I have learned if I have too much down time?

On the first day of our swim course, my cousin and I showed up early. This was the result of a strategic approach I had developed based on my previous experience: arrive on site well before the others in order to have time to look around, get to know the instructors, obtain useful information and then relax and watch the arrival of the crowds panicked by the chaos of the first day.

Upon arriving at the front desk, we proudly showed our membership card to the staff, grabbed a hanger and entered the locker room. We were slightly excited, as if this were our first day of school. We joked around and revisited memories of Boy Scout camps, summer beach vacations and my history of water intolerance. As we arrived on deck, we looked like anything but athletes, donning swim shorts pulled up to our bellybutton, terry robes two sizes too large and dorky-looking rubber flip-flops. As we proceeded to the gym, we patiently waited for the others to arrive. We waited for a few minutes, but nothing happened. We began wondering whether we had showed up on the wrong day or at the wrong place. Finally, one instructor and six more participants arrived, a few at a time. Then, surrounded by an atmosphere that felt completely distressing and surreal compared to my recent past, we began our warm-up exercises. I inquired by asking: "Did the others know that the swim course started today?" The instructor replied, "This class is not full. Based on my attendance sheet, we only have two absent today." I asked myself whether that was a positive or negative thing, but I decided to wait until the end of the swim lesson to answer my own question.

Once we entered the water, we were assigned two out of a total of six lanes and one instructor. The shallow water level throughout the pool allowed us to remain standing while the instructor talked to us, instead of floating around like ducklings. The only item that created a little disturbance was the water aerobics course being held in the adjacent lanes. While dancing to the tunes of typical disco songs, which, due to the poor acoustics of the facility, felt like our ears were being slapped, a dozen out-of-shape ladies vigorously shook the water generating freak waves that defied any laws of physics in the hope to burn as many calories as possible. Useless to say, the targets mostly hit by those massive waves were the wide-open mouths of the rest of us unfortunate swimmers as we breathed between strokes. Despite the unfavorable environmental conditions, within a month I improved my abilities and reached the much-coveted goal of swimming forty laps in a single lesson. What made this goal fascinating was that, in physical terms, this meant having swum a whole kilometer!

From a teaching point of view, in addition to perfecting freestyle, backstroke and breaststroke, the course included an introduction to butterfly, the stroke that everyone loves to watch and nobody wants to swim as it requires extreme physical effort. As shown in the swim manual, the first step was to learn the dolphin kick. They explained that in this stroke the leg movement is the same as that in freestyle, except the flutter kick is replaced by a new kick, in which legs kick together like the fin of a mermaid. As I listened to the instructor, I thought back to the previous year when I was still fighting to master my breaststroke and I used my time underwater to observe my fellow swimmers move as mermaids. I remembered myself saying something like, "Hey, that's Patrick Duffy... and there is one more over there... and another one over there!" as I recalled that actor who starred in the eighties' television series Man from Atlantis. I woke up and tuned into what the instructor was saying, although by then he was finished explaining the exercise. I took my time and let the others go ahead of me to watch what they did to better understand what underwater work meant and how to only move your legs as if they were a fin. When I thought I understood, I concluded that keeping your arms stretched out over your head and moving your bottom up and down cannot be that difficult. After a few seconds I was forced to change my mind, especially when I found myself hitting the bottom of the pool with my head. I swam back to the surface, took a deep breath and tried again, but the outcome was the same: instead of moving horizontally, I ended up swimming to the bottom. Somebody explained to me that this was not caused by the shallow water level, but rather that it was a consequence of my stance, which was decisively too curvy to advance on a straight line. By keeping my back straight and a trajectory parallel to the surface of the water, I should be able to swim a lap like the others. Maybe so, however, even maintaining a correct posture, after a few leg strokes I felt overwhelmed by fatigue and the need to stop and rest.

Once we began working on the arm movement, things got even worse. We began by using the pull-buoy. A pull-buoy is a small floating device shaped like the number 8. You hold it on the inside of your legs (right above your thighs/knees) and it allows you to swim using only your upper body. I cannot begin to describe how fond I am of this item because, when I use it, I can eliminate almost all of my drag. However, as opposed to freestyle, where using a pull-buoy is a relaxing activity, using just your arms for the butterfly is tiring. This happens because, by using your hands simultaneously, you have no rest time like you do when you swim freestyle.

After a few lessons spent trying to perform separate arm and leg strokes, one fateful day our instructor invited us to combine the two movements and see what happens. On my first attempt, I felt like I was moving backwards, even though I was moving forward! There was something very wrong in what I did, not only because I could not advance at all, but also because I could only keep up with this physical effort for just a few seconds, rather than for an entire lap.

I began to ask myself if this was my learning limit in sports and my personal best in swimming. Doing the butterfly seemed to be such a complicated and difficult stroke that I began feeling profoundly useless and incompetent. Just as my thoughts began feeling like a limiting conviction, one night those swimmers taking courses in the next level up showed me how to win the most daring challenge of my life…

My eyesight is not the best: I am nearsighted and even a little astigmatic. My eyesight issues are not serious; however, when I am in the pool, anything that lies beyond one meter from my nose looks out of focus, loses detail and its outline is out of focus.
One evening, at the end of our latest lesson on the

butterfly, my eyesight was more blurry than usual due to my being tired. What is more is that I had no energy left and I did not feel like leaping out of the pool as I usually do. I felt like I needed to use the pool ladder. I swam across the lap. As I reached the metal steps, I noticed that the participants of the following swim session were using that ladder to enter the water. In fact, some of them were already swimming. I moved closer to see what they did and I squeezed my eyes. I could not see very well, but I noticed that they swam vigorously, looking full of energy and extremely vital. Compared to them, I felt like I held the power of a newborn baby during his baby bath.

I grabbed the ladder and turned to the water to observe them for a little while. I focused on them and, all of a sudden, I remembered the wheelchairs and prostheses laying around the lockers in the locker room, and, for some reason, I had thought that they belonged to those using the nearby gym, not swimmers. Conversely, those devices were what allowed those swimmers to move freely outside the water, as many of them had lost their extremities or full use of their legs.

My eyesight is not the best; however, that night I was able to see with extreme clarity how human beings can conquer even their most difficult daily challenges when they have the will, determination and desire to live.

After a spending a month teaching us, our instructor had to quit his job for personal reasons. He was replaced by another instructor who was very qualified and nice, although a bit less charismatic. ·I am not sure if this was the cause of the apparent drop in attendance that followed. It was not unusual for my cousin and me to be the only two swimmers in our lane and, although having the entire lane at your disposal was nice, the lack of competition turned out to be demotivating. At the end of the semester, I switched to the pool near my house, which I found to be very lively. My cousin, as lazy as can be, preferred not to follow me, so he said, "You can try it out, and maybe I will join you next year." The funny thing is that my new swimming pool was the same one where I had my first swimming experience as a child. When I went there to sign up, Luca, a nice and thoughtful course coordinator, suggested that I should consider the Masters level course. It was the first time that I had heard of such a thing in swimming, so I stood there feeling perplexed, yet the thought of it was fascinating. In order to attend the Masters level course, swimmers must first meet two requirements: they must be able to swim an entire lap in each of the four strokes and have the endurance to swim ten laps non-stop. To avoid all uncertainty, I signed up for a more laid-back advanced course, delaying the Masters experience until the following year. On the day of our first lesson, I was greeted by the nicest and most beautiful instructor I had ever seen; plus, she was always happy, smiling and attentive to correct any minor errors; plus she did very well in the water. I gathered this by observing her teaching method, which, unusually, did not consist of an unending flow of words; in fact, her verbal instructions were backed up by precious in-water demonstrations. Every time she entered the water with us, I tried to retain as much information as possible, alternating views from above and from inside the water, as if I was a movie director working on a documentary. I was surprised to see how her body glided through water instead of looking like she was fighting against it, which is the way we looked. Her movements were harmonious, calm and precise. After a few strokes, she reached an impressive speed, thanks to which she completed a lap in just few seconds. Her kicks were slow yet powerful, and they looked more like strokes of fins than kicking feet. What seemed inexplicable was that, while doing all this, she did not seem to have exerted herself at all, but rather like she was running on special propulsion fuel. At the end of her demonstrations, our jaws dropped, our eyes were wide open and everyone exploded in a resounding, well-deserved applause.

In addition to the pleasure felt by admiring so much sports beauty, my mind was filled with a mixed thoughts, wishes, expectations and fears. I wanted to swim like that, but I was not sure if I would ever learn. I wanted to have her fluidity, but I didn't think that it was a skill that I could easily acquire. I was sure that, by continuing to press forward, sooner or later I would learn to swim better; however, I was convinced that I would never reach her level. In other words, simple teaching demonstrations generated deep reflections about my possibilities and personal limits.

ANALYSIS – Limits and thereabouts

Limits draw the line between what you can do and what you think you cannot do. In order to understand the mechanics of limits and what effect they have on you, try to imagine the following situation...

It is summer time. You are at the beach. It is late in the afternoon and the weather is nice. Your beach umbrella is closed: pull the umbrella out of the sand, remove the bottom pole and, without additional directions, I invite you to use it to draw a circle around you. Without any hesitation, you remain where you are and, as you rotate around yourself, you do as you are told by tracing a circle of more or less the diameter of your arm extended by the length of the pole. Now I would like for you to look closely at your circle and your position compared to it: you'll notice that you are inside a circle that defines what is within your reach and what is out of your reach, which is just a few steps away. The interesting thing is that I never said that you had to stand still while you drew your circle; I only asked, in very specific words, to "draw a circle in the sand around you." You could have drawn a circle by walking for hours while remaining inside it; conversely, you performed the task using the least amount of energy for a comfortable average outcome. Test it on a friend, but make sure to use my exact words: "Take the pole and trace a circle on the sand around you." Rarely does anybody push herself to do something different from what I just described.

Let's get back to us. You are now standing in the middle of the circle that you just traced on the sand. Imagine that this circle represents the perimeter of your limits, the border between what you know how to do, which is inside the circle with you, and what you don't know how to do, which is beyond the line. Now step outside of this picture and imagine looking in at yourself in this situation: you look like a little dot inside a small circle, surrounded by an immense expanse of sand. That small dot is you. The circle represents your limits. The beach represents the infinite range of possibilities for human beings.

If you tell yourself that you cannot go beyond that circle or broaden its borders, then you are destined to remain bound by your limits. By all means, this is an easy situation to be in because you are not forced to get moving, make an effort, overexert yourself, break a sweat or live actively; however, keep in mind that you are not in this situation because destiny tragically unleashed it against you, but rather it is mainly the result of a personal decision. That's right; it is your decision to stand still and limit yourself to always do the same things in the same way, cheating yourself with the typical loser's statements such as "I can't do it" or "I am not capable." However, if you decide to put forth an effort, then you can broaden your possibilities, just as many others do. Your only true destiny is to grow, even if this requires energy and effort, because growing is in the nature of all living things on earth: plants, animals and human beings; if you are not growing, then you are dying. Every being on earth needs to continue to grow, mature over time and gradually broaden its circle because otherwise this would mean that she is giving up on life.

Your body needs to exercise and be stimulated to keep from wasting away. Neurons, the cells inside your brain, are a bit like small people inside your head: if they have nothing new to tell, they begin experiencing loneliness and suffering and, sooner or later, they let themselves die. Your muscles need exercise; otherwise they will begin to waste away. You work just like a plant: as long as there is light, your branches will grow toward it will even change shape to live. You don't get to pick where you are born or whether your birth place is in a sunny or shady area, but you can decide to fight to reach the light or remain in the darkness that has befallen on you and let yourself die.

Just like me and everyone else, you have a need to grow, to gradually exceed your limits, refusing to accept your current capabilities as set in stone and learning to do something new. The issue is that human beings have the strange tendency to shell up inside a small circle and remain in there as they prefer enjoying the comfort of their present laziness rather than investing energy to earn great future joy. This is a mechanism that can become the end of you: if your mind is convinced that what it sees is all true, then your organism adapts to this belief and ends up reducing its abilities to match those set limits, being convinced that it cannot do much more than that. If your decision is to sit still within a set perimeter, then your mind delivers this limitation to your body, which becomes used to limiting itself and to only do what this small view of reality allows it to do. Your body ends up like a dog chained to its kennel, which, by remaining confined to a small area, ends up believing that the world is what it sees around it.

Another thing is also true. The decisions that you take to limit your world are in part, but only in part, a normal process to keep you from going insane. This allows you to simplify reality and live with others, without having to reinvent or renegotiate everything on a daily basis (relationships, language, the way you get things done, etc.) For example, this is inevitable in social relationships, which are affected by routines and rules that crystallize interactions into predictable situations allowing you to act by taking many things for granted. You also take it for granted that if you say hello to someone and you say, "how is it going?" she will say, "I am doing well or not so well," rather than "how is what going?" and that if you are in a classroom to attend a lesson, the attendees will sit quietly and listen to the teacher, rather than walk around and chat, asking why they should pay attention to the person sitting behind the desk. This process of simplification is also activated within relationships, so rather than investing time in getting to know a person well, it can happen that you'll limit yourself to quickly label this person. Therefore so and so becomes "your best friend," Joe Bloggs becomes "a pain in the neck," Joe Soap is the "busybody" and so on. Despite their individual assets and complexity, in your mind, people around you become simple characters in a movie (that of your life) to which you have assigned a role (the label) solely based on one aspect of their character that you have decided to see in her (virtue or flaw). This process of simplification happens without you being aware of it and this may potentially drive you to running on autopilot, which, although on one hand this is a functional aspect of your existence, on the other hand it may dramatically reduce your possibilities. Certainly, rules are necessary to coexist with others; however, using them in an uncritical way will lead you to believe things that may not entirely be true. For example, you may think that certain common beliefs are true only because most people think it is so.

Tens of years ago, a not-so-tall guy realized that playing basketball was very challenging and very demanding for him; in fact, it required a huge effort. When he looked around, he noticed that others could achieve better results without overexerting themselves because the basket was closer to their hands than his. So, in order to conceal his lack of will to increase his efforts and to retreat without anyone calling him a loser, he began to say, "Basketball is for tall people... it's the rules!" This sentence began to spread by word of mouth. Tall people used it to discourage short people and short people used it to justify their failures...

In this way, the sentence "basketball is for tall people" has become an unquestionable rule; in fact, if you are short and play basketball, you can use it to justify yourself by using this universally accepted rule every time you have trouble recovering or throwing the ball. Beware: abiding by such a rule is both convenient and terribly devastating because following it means accepting a small and skimpy circle of possibilities. Remember one thing: every time a tall basketball player fails at recovering and throwing the ball, he does not say, "I have physical limitations," but rather he attributes his failure to a lack of ability that may be improved by practicing. Then, what would happen if this kind of response were also used by a short player?

Tyrone Curtis Bogues was born in Baltimore on January 9, 1965. He was raised in an area of the city where

drugs and guns were the norm and where many must use them to ensure their own survival. Tyrone spent much of his free time playing basketball, a sport that he loved and for which he felt he had a gift. When he was all grown up, Tyrone was only 5 foot 3 inches tall so, unlike taller guys, he was unable to dunk as he could only throw. Despite that, he was profoundly convinced that he had what it took to become a great champion. In his heart he knew that he was exceptionally talented for this sport. Tyrone believed in himself, always and incessantly, so at the age of 22 he succeeded in becoming a professional, making history as the shortest American NBA player. This was possible only because Muggsy, that was his nickname, never regarded his height as an issue, refusing to accept the commonplace, "basketball is a sport for very tall people." He always trusted himself, his will to succeed and express his talent, which he never doubted. Thanks to his faith in himself, not only did he gain entrance in the most important basketball league in the world, but he also succeeded in blocking thirty-nine throws shot by opponents who were decisively taller than him. His feats include his historical block (this is the technical term to indicate that the ball that someone just threw to the basket and that is still just few inches from the shooter's hand is hit or stopped by the intervention of a defense player) against Patrick Ewing, a 7-foot tall opponent, who is among the top-fifty best players of the NBA.

Tyrone Curtis Bogues never used phrases like: "It's impossible or I can't do it." Tyrone always told himself, "I believe in myself".

"What happens often times" in your head can become "what happens all the time," so instead of testing your true limits, you can end up believing things you hear through the grapevine, accepting limitations spread by others.

Who knows how many times you have given up doing something after a few tries only because you just used a small part of your potential as you were convinced that "you would have never succeeded." Who knows how many times you refrained from putting all your heart, will and soul in what you were doing, not truly convincing yourself that you could do it. All those times, my friend, you cheated yourself because if you were truly convinced of your possibilities, then nothing and nobody could have kept you from reaching your goals...

Natalie is a girl from South Africa. Before she turned six, she had no desire to spend any time in the water. In fact, her relationship with the water was one of the worst anyone could imagine. Although this may seem unconceivable, Natalie ended up developing a passion for swimming and, within a few years, it became her reason to live, so much so that, at the age of sixteen, Natalie almost qualified for the 2000 Sydney Olympics. In her heart, she knew that it was just a matter of time because she was truly convinced that she had what it takes to be a champion. On February 26, 2001, Natalie began her day like any other day: she woke up very early, ate breakfast and went to the pool for morning practice. When you are training as an advanced swimmer, your daily routine includes waking up at the crack of dawn, having a light breakfast and a challenging practice before school; then in the afternoons you return to the pool for a second practice. This is what it means to be professional athlete, and Natalie is a professional. That day, just like many others, Natalie left the swimming pool and headed toward school. All of a sudden, a car hit her with unconceivable brutality; it was truly a miracle that she survived and only ended up losing

her left leg. Her trauma was very intense, both physically and psychologically, as well as hard enough to break anyone's spirit. Natalie was not the type of person who gave up easily, not even when faced with such a life-changing situation so, instead of giving up, after her recovery she returned to the pool, began practicing again and, day by day, rebuilt her career from scratch. As she returned to swimming, she must adapt to her new capabilities. Her motivation was all in her heart, mind and soul. Stroke after stroke, practice after practice, Natalie regained her outstanding shape and returned to competing against her able-bodied peers. The only thing that changed was the event: instead of competing in short-distance events, she participated in long distance races, such as the 800- meter and 1500-meter freestyle, distances on which legwork has a lower impact.

In 2002, a year after her accident, Natalie participated in the Commonwealth Games. She reached the finals for the 800-meter freestyle and she barely missed placing third. However, she later succeeded in 2003, when she earned a landmark gold medal in the 800 meter freestyle. In 2008, at the age of 24, Natalie Du Toit achieved the dream of her life by qualifying for the Peking Olympics in the 10 kilometer long-distance swim in open waters.

In preparation for this event, she trained with effort and commitment, always believing in herself and never hiding behind the fact that she was missing one leg. In fact, on the day of the race, as soon as the judge declared the start of the competition, Natalie did not shy away from the free for all that took place on the beach at the beginning of the race, where athletes with no assigned lanes to separate them were physically in contact with each other. The race was an elbow-to-elbow competition and Natalie led the way with many other rivals while keeping up with the leading group for a long time. Worn out by fatigue, Natalie came in thirteenth out of twenty-five, with a net time of two hours. Her achievement was more than honorable, and to the eyes of millions of television viewers around the world, it simply looked like a miracle, but her big heart yearned for more. Then, looking back at her endeavors, during one of her countless interviews Natalie told her story: "I remember that on the day of my accident, people screamed at the sight of my leg. Then I remember the great effort it took to rebuild my muscle mass also due to my thigh bone shattering in multiple points. I am convinced that all this has not weakened me, but it has made me stronger. In fact, it is possible that with two healthy legs I would have never made it to the Olympics. People tend to focus too much on the past and the things they have lost. I came to realize that those things do not come back and that you cannot do anything about that; however, many new things come to you and they deserve to be experienced".

Your limits are those you set for yourself, often on the basis of information delivered by others for who knows what reason. To overcome your limits, you must learn to trust the information that comes from within you and quit relying on ready-made phrases or weakening advice. For once in your life, do something odd and unusual: close your eyes and visualize your circle of limits that you drew around you. Try to use the inner you to redefine it, and this time let it be what you want. Then the circle will appear larger and full of possibilities. Having faith in yourself is essential to reach your goals. If you feel like you do not have self-esteem, do not despair: you can build it. How? First of all, change your attitude and try to seize the positive aspects of what happens in your life. But there's more. To find out, all you have to do is read the next chapter.

EMOTION
Wolf or man?

In India, an infant was abandoned in the forest. Instead of tearing the baby to pieces, the wolf took him in and raised him. The child grew and became an adult; however, he continued to live like a wolf, always walking on all fours. He was fast, efficiently used his sense of smell and he even developed sharp teeth, just like a wolf. Then, one day he ran into a strange creature. He looked at the creature defiantly and got ready to attack if it turned out to be dangerous. But the creature left without even noticing his presence. The wolf child asked his mother what was that tall creature: strong, white and walking erect on two legs. His mother told him that the creature was a man, the most dangerous and powerful species that existed on earth. For a moment, the child thought that he would like to be a man but then he realized how absurd his dream was. He erased his dream from his mind and resigned himself to live as a wolf for the rest of his life.

EXERCISE

This is an excellent exercise to get used to doing without those limits that derive from other people's statements.

1. Take a day to carefully listen to the words of people that surround you and the phrases they use.

2. Pay attention every time they say things like, "I am not able," "I can't," "it's not possible," "I couldn't manage," and so on.

3. When faced with a statement of this kind, ask yourself the following question: "What is really keeping them from doing what they say they can't do?" Depending on the relationship that you have with them, ask them that question, if possible.

4. Now put yourself in their shoes and imagine that their limit is your limit. What would you do to overcome that limit?

5. Try to repeat this exercise a few times in order to understand how often human beings limit themselves.

CHAPTER 5: MASTERS SWIMMING

EXPERIENCE – The winning response

When I first signed up for the first swimming course for adults, I had no clue what my new endeavor would lead to, also because my sole concern at the time was to just get active, transitioning from a state of inactivity to a state of motion. Once I got moving, I began living day by day, trying to survive each lesson. I would have never thought that my swimming adventure would go on for a third consecutive year or that I would improve my performance by overcoming many challenges; nonetheless I did it, proving my ability to persevere as well as my strong sense of determination. This positive state of mind brought on increased confidence, so I told myself that I had reached the crossroads and that it was time to raise the bar by attempting something different. Therefore, when I was again invited to sign up for Masters swimming, I accepted without hesitation, displaying that plastic smile stamped on the face of those who make a choice having no idea what their choice entails and hoping that they won't regret it.

On the day of my first lesson, I found out that those extremely boring warm-up exercises were no longer a requirement and that the sixty-minute lesson was entirely dedicated to in-pool training. This was a welcome change also because I had always believed that the sole purpose of dryland training was to burn one-third of my energy.

The second thing I noticed was that the average age of the participants was lower than in my previous courses. Apart from a man in his fifties and a couple of guys in their thirties, our group was primarily made up of young people aged eighteen to twenty-four and a couple of girls slightly past their teenage years. The atmosphere was lively: everyone knew everyone; they laughed together and were especially at ease with each other. The instructor, the only one for the entire group, was nice and confident as if he were a very seasoned entertainer. He reminded me of the famous officer Poncherello, from the renowned TV series CHiPs.

There was so much chatter going on that some got too wrapped up in their conversations and forgot to get in the pool when it was time to begin. I, on the other hand, took a good look around to figure out who went into each of the four lanes to quickly identify where I belonged, based on my abilities. It turned out to be a challenging task. When I realized that I was the only one still standing outside the swimming pool, I quit hesitating and I got into the lane next to the girls': lane two.

Our first assignment is to warm up by swimming twenty consecutive laps. As odd as this may seem, I had never swum that many laps without stopping for as long as I had been swimming; at any rate, I avoided any unnecessary scary thoughts and focused my attention on the fact that this was only the beginning and that my strength was still intact. A few laps later I realized that, by taking this course, I could get screwed in various unexpected ways, such as, for example, by being continuously doubled by the other swimmers in my lane, who seemed to belong to an alien race.

At the end of this first lively warm-up, I hardly had time

to recover before we were told to swim a dozen more laps aimed at improving our technique. The assigned exercises were the usual ones: swim one lap with one arm and one lap with the other one. However, what struck me was that everyone was in a big hurry to finish their tasks. At the end of this second set of laps, I felt physically and mentally ready to exit the pool and go take a shower, so I headed for the ladder. As I got ready to leave, the instructor's words stopped me in my tracks: "Alright, now that you are warmed up, let's begin our workout. This set includes: one lap backstroke, one lap breaststroke and one lap freestyle. Repeat ten times, resting 15-seconds between sets." For a moment, I stood there struggling to comprehend what I had just heard; then, resigned and fearful, I went back to join the group. Just as before, the action was frenzied, the breaks were very short and the number of laps was excessive for human beings equipped with only one heart. I got doubled once, twice and three times, although I was giving it my all and, at this point, I was breathing as loudly as a vacuum cleaner. Just when I thought that my heart was just about ready to come out of my chest, I decided that it was time to stop and get some rest, which I did with the blessing of my instructor, who seemed to understand my state as he motioned to take it easy. If this weren't enough to make me feel like the biggest loser, I looked over at my fellow swimmers and, for a moment, I hallucinated that they had all developed strange-looking fins on their backs.

At the end the lesson, I struggled to pull myself out the pool, so I practiced self-hypnosis by repeating: "I may falter, but I will not fall." This technique worked and it allowed me to arrive to the locker room; then, all of a sudden, my knees began to shake, which was a sign that they were approaching structural failure. With a feline-like leap, I successfully landed on the first available bench; then, I raised my legs by setting them up against the wall and I began to take deep, long breaths. Somebody asked if I was feeling okay and I replied that I was just having a moment and that I would soon feel better, knowing fully well that I was lying through my teeth. In my head, I kept thinking one thing, which more or less sounded like, "Antonio, what type of course did you sign up for?!?" The following lessons confirmed my conviction that I was the wrong person in the wrong place, and my instructor also realized that, so he very tactfully suggested that I should consider moving to the girls' lane so I could set pace for them. In reality, although the setting had changed, the outcome had remained the same because, although the girls swam more slowly than their male counterparts, I was still the last one to go and the first one to break down. I could hold my own on only one task: sprinting over short distances. The most popular exercise included sprinting for one-half lap, alternating with rest periods of approximately twenty seconds. The incredible thing was that, during that brief sprint, I could swim almost as quickly as the others. I didn't know how this came about or where all my energy came from; all I knew is that it was happening and I was happy about it. If just I didn't feel so worn out at the end of each practice...

As time went on, I began experiencing increasing difficulty going to sleep at night. The same situation kept recurring: I swam, ate and went to bed only to find myself staring at the ceiling for hours, listening to the frantic beating of my heart and feeling extremely hot, regardless of the outside temperature. Someone told me that these symptoms may be caused by swim training, while others said that it happens to those who practice for the first time. I calmed down once I realized that others were experiencing the same thing, so I decided to classify the disturbance as a sign of good training and I quit noticing it.

Months went by and I overcame moments of weakness, accepting my temporary role as the tail-end swimmer of the Masters course. The only thing that kept me going was my desire to see how this adventure would end, also because I was determined to stay the course, unless someone told me that I had to switch to a course better suited for my abilities. So I continued attending the Masters swim course through the winter and over the following summer, participating in resistance and speed training, including the most extravagant and unexpected workouts...

When the instructor asked us to bring a T-shirt to practice, I immediately thought that this was a nice gesture on his part. Since I care about my health, I faithfully followed his advice and arrived at the pool wearing a size XL T-shirt. With pleasure, I noticed that even the others had brought their T-shirts: some were red, some were white, some were large and some were small. For a moment I had a wild thought: "What if the instructor asked us to swim wearing our T-shirts?" I laughed at the odd thoughts that pop up in my head from time to time, then, to kill time I began warming up my face muscles by chatting with those standing around me.When the instructor arrived, he was shirtless as usual: he truly enjoyed showing off his sculpted marble abs. However, this time he looked different. It took me a little while to figure out that his facial expression was different and a little while more to pinpoint that his was the expression of those who enjoy watching others suffer. He looked at us and said, "Good job, guys; everyone brought in their T-shirt! Tonight you will swim with it!" One of my fellow swimmers promptly asked, "What do you mean?" The instructor replied, "I mean that you will enter the water while keeping your T-shirt on." Everyone was quiet. To avoid looking like a chicken, I behaved like, in my extensive swimming experience, I had done a million things like that. The instructor added, "...swimming with a T-shirt improves one's water perception. This is how it works: You'll swim for about one-half hour wearing your T-shirt. You will naturally feel slower, heavier and clumsy. Then, you will remove your T-shirt to feel light, fast and flowing." I was speechless; this instructor was really good: not only did he tell us what we need to do and how, but also why.

I entered the pool and I began swimming with my shirt on. I first felt like I was dragging something along, which reminded me of those horrible nightmares in which, despite desperate attempts, you cannot move or escape as desired. Slowly, and with great effort for half an hour, I performed low-impact exercises. Some exercises made me feel wobbly, while others make me long for swimming the butterfly. The weight of the fabric felt heavier as we swam more laps. I felt like I was dragging a heavy load and I was constantly out of balance. When our instructor told us to remove our shirt, I didn't make him say it twice. I removed my drenched shirt, wrapped it into a big ball and I set it on the edge of the pool. Then I took a deep breath to relax my muscles before going back to swimming.

I began swimming again. All of a sudden, I had the impression that I was as light as a feather and moving along the edge of the water felt easy now. As I paid closer attention to my body, I noticed something else: my skin felt cool; in fact, for the first time I felt water flow down my back and chest, sensing it as a friendly rather than menacing presence. Not bad. I must say that the exercise worked and that I had received the gift of awareness.

Swimming while wearing a T-shirt is one of many exercises aimed at gaining awareness of the aspects that affect buoyancy and energy savings in swimming. During another practice, our instructor made us swim while holding plastic bottles full of water. In addition to making my muscles look like the incredible Hulk's, that workout made me realize that:

1. your hand is not the only part of your upper body that pulls water during your stroke;
2. even your forearm plays a relevant role, even though you may not feel it pulling;
3. kicking is not only useful for advancing, but also to maintain your horizontal balance (your kicks actually help keep your legs up, which would otherwise float to the bottom);
4. recovery of the arm bent with your fingers moving near the body takes less effort than stretching out your arm.

Another interesting experience involved alternating workouts in the water with dryland exercises. This vaguely reminded me of a military training course: we gathered in the yard past the sliding glass doors by the pool, an area that is commonly used to lie out in the sun. We were instructed to jump over obstacles, crawl on the ground, do sit-ups and push-ups; then we had to rush back to the pool and swim four laps of freestyle. We had to repeat this series for countless times and this reminded me of Wild Boys, an oldie music video by Duran Duran, in which lead singer Simon Le Bon was tied to an enormous torture wheel and repeatedly exposed to water and fire.

These summer workouts brought us to the end of the course, and I must say that this was the best and most fun course that I had ever attended. However, on the first day of my fourth year of swimming, after returning from summer vacation, I sadly realized that many things had changed: new pool coordinator, new swim instructor and even new swimmers; all the familiar faces from the previous year had disappeared, but what is worse was that nobody seemed to want to explain ("Who? What? Never heard of him... are you sure?") I found myself attending a Masters swimming course that had nothing in common with the previous one, except the name. The second course took place in a single lane, with six participants and one instructor; the latter was regularly replaced by a new instructor every two months. That year went by most boringly to the point that, for the first time since I had been swimming, I felt like I had made no improvement. The only interesting experience from that course was the end-of-the-year competition, AKA the first competition of my life. This event was held by the Milan city pools to celebrate the end of swim season. Each swimmer may choose to participate in one or two out of four competitions, which included one lap butterfly, one lap backstroke, one lap breaststroke or one lap freestyle. I choose freestyle and butterfly...

So there I was, in the hallway of the Cozzi swimming pool. The ceiling was very high. For a moment, I thought that giants and wading birds would not have any trouble standing in that place. I looked around and I felt my heart plunging. This was the first time that I had set foot into this facility; however, something felt familiar. I tried to remember; then all of a sudden I had a flashback...

I was about 6 years old. I was at this swimming pool with my father; we were standing behind the double glass wall that looks into the 33 meter pool. I was watching my brother taking swim lessons. I gazed on horrified by the idea that fun could be linked to water, feeling a bit vindicated when I noticed that, as I expected, many children were crying because they felt cold. On the other hand, my brother swam and had fun: it really looked like he enjoyed being in the water. Then my memory skipped forward and I found myself in front of a large porthole in the underground level. We were still there, watching the swimmers, but my perspective was different: this time I was standing below water level, in front of what appeared to be a large human aquarium. My father explained that this lower level was used when the pool hosted diving competitions...

The word "competition" brought me back from my state of hypnosis and made me snap out of my trance. I shook myself and headed to the locker room. In the locker room, I sat on a bench and put on my bathing suit, robe and deck shoes. I visualized my upcoming events. My thoughts focused on my upcoming butterfly event and I was unsure if I could complete it.

I arrived poolside, feeling preoccupied and hesitant. All sections of the bleachers were full. I looked around the audience to locate my friends, but I stood in the same place for too long and the event organizers told me to go take a seat on the stands. I was pleasantly surprised to find out that among these caring staff members was the long-lost nice coordinator from last year. I looked astonished and said hello; he responded in his typical ironic tone, "What are you doing here? You know, there is no practice today." I smiled and asked why everyone changed jobs. He mentioned that some management issues affected his decision; however, he did not know what had happened to the others. Then, he explained how this swim meet worked: each event comprised one heat and the first three swimmers to place in each heat would win a medal. I got excited and started thinking that I could possibly win a medal in my freestyle event. However, what mattered most was making it through my butterfly event.

After waiting for about one hour, it was my turn. When I heard them marshaling my name, I behaved like the typical guy who releases tension by cracking a joke. Two other swimmers and I lined up for the last heat of the butterfly event and, since there were only three of us, I immediately realized that all three would receive a medal. As my confidence rose, I decided not to take any chances and I mentally planned to swim prudently and with the sole goal of completing the lap. I headed toward the starting block and put on my goggles. I placed them tightly on my face because I did not want them to come off during the dive: that would truly be a terrible loss. I was very nervous, but, at the same time, I was having fun. At "take your marks," I bent over and grabbed the edge of my starting block with the tips of my fingers; then, at the start signal, I leaped into the water gliding on my belly. The transition from outside to inside the water happened so quickly that I felt like my eyesight had turned foggy. It took a few moments for me to realize that my goggles had flipped up on my forehead. I couldn't see anything: there was water everywhere and my eyes were burning. Although I was almost in a panic, I began doing the butterfly. After a few meters past my dive, I began feeling extremely tired due to my swimming blindly and uncoordinatedly: I could no longer pull my arms out of the water during the recovery phase and I began to swallow water. I tried to open my eyes to figure out what was happening, but the chlorine stung, allowing me to hold out just long enough to see that, unless I was delirious, my competitors looked like they were approaching the end of the race. I was still half way down the lane and I realized that there must have been about two hundred people watching my struggle. I tried to work on my pride and intensify the action, but my performance was disappointing. I broke down and swallowed more pool water; then I realized that my arms were no longer moving, so I decided to quit the race by swimming freestyle the rest of the way. As I exited the pool, I felt down and out because I was sure that I had been disqualified. I walked past the podium: my opponents were already standing on the first two steps. I looked over sadly, so one of the event organizers invited me to take the third place. Then he added, "You know, this wasn't a mixed stroke event! Here's your medal." Although unsatisfied by my performance, I felt confused, yet happy for having received my unexpected prize; I reset my mind and focused on my next event.

When it was time for my freestyle event, my name was marshaled in a heat full of participants, so, this time around the only way to earn a medal was to fight for it. And that was fine by me because, if I were to succeed, I would feel redeemed from my recent embarrassing moment. I approached my starting block, and this time I made sure to tighten my goggles as much as humanly possible. I tried to concentrate by repeating the following sentence: "Breathe as little as possible and spin away." I climbed on the starting block and prepared to dive. When the starting official gave the signal, I jumped into the water and I gave it my all. This time my goggles did not move an inch. Looking out of the corner of my eye, I realized that I was head to head with the other contestants, and my position remained unchanged half way down the lap. Over the last few meters things changed as I ended the race one-half length behind the winners. We all rushed to the finish and quickly touched the wall, one by one. Once the official times were released, I saw that I had placed well below third place, which made me feel a bit disappointed. However, my disappointment was shortly lived as I mainly felt excited for having participated in such an event. I sighed and sat up straight. I felt a deep sense of accomplishment. Then I said something unusual, which sounded a bit like this: "Ah, wouldn't it be so nice to participate in many meets?"

ANALYSIS - The importance of reacting as an adult

When you try to do something and you don't succeed, you probably feel like you have failed. And if you have failed, then it follows that you are a failure. If you think you are a failure, you will begin feeling like a failure, acting like a failure and taking home more failures.

Neurolinguistics researchers have performed studies on the links between linguistics and mental activities, ascertaining that one entails the other and vice-versa. The effects produced by such links are surprising: the use of positive words enables your mind to find solutions to your problems, broadens your perspective and, more generally, sets you up for growth; conversely, the use of negative words relegates your mind to dark places that provide no solutions, produce a chain reaction of disasters and keep human beings from growing. If you wish to take a look at these studies, take your pick: libraries are full of excellent titles. Next, I will introduce some basic ideas so that, through the use of immediate examples, you can understand how the process works and how you can immediately put winning strategies into practice to overcome difficult moments in your swimming and non-swimming career.

Let's begin from the following premise: your brain is that organ whose job is to process information in order to draw conclusions. It works almost like a calculator. If you take a calculator and key in 1 + 1 followed by the "equals" sign, you result will be the positive number +2. Conversely, if you key in –1 – 1, your result will be the negative number – 2. Now, your brain is not exactly a calculator; however, it moves along the same lines: if your thoughts, inner monologues (the things you say to yourself) and the questions you ask yourself are positive thoughts, then your conclusions will also be positive; conversely, if you think negative thoughts, your conclusions will also be negative. And that's not all.

There are people who, based on experience and education, are geared to have negative reactions when facing life situations, even when these may potentially be positive experiences. They are people who tend to see the glass half-empty, rather than half full, therefore if someone gives them a book, they will think, "okay, but that's not the book I wanted," or if they guess five of the lottery winning numbers, they will think, "okay, but I could have guessed all six." In addition to never being happy, these people have the tendency to only talk about the negative things they have experienced. As I just mentioned, your brain is like a calculator, so if you say negative things, you will reach negative conclusions, which will make your state of mind and inner self rot away. Let me give you an example.

If you keep telling yourself that your boss does not give you the time of the day, your brain may conclude that: "It's obvious that he does not give you the time of the day: he is an idiot!" This conclusion would lead you to treat him like an idiot, making you adopt hostile behavior around him. When feeling attacked, it is obvious that your boss would resent your attitude and not pay any attention to you, fueling a vicious cycle that may potentially have explosive results.

When faced with the same situation, if instead of reacting automatically, you stop and analyze what is happening in a positive way, maybe by telling yourself that your boss would treat you better if he knew how good you are, then your brain could conclude the following: "Well, then you should show him what you can do," or: "Meet his expectations, after understanding what those are."

If you want to change the outcomes in your life to keep away painful feelings, you must make an effort to redefine your thoughts in order to make them analytical and positive, instead of automatically negative. Changing your reactions takes a concerted effort, that's for sure; however, you can do it, also because pressing positive buttons rather than negative ones depends entirely on you. To succeed, you must avoid excuses that justify laziness, such as: "This is my character; that's the way I am and there is nothing I can do about it!" Although it may be true that this is just the way you are, it is not true that you cannot do anything about it: everything comes from decisions that you can change whenever you want. I will take it one step further to better explain myself.

When you do something and you don't obtain the outcome that you expect, you always have a choice: you can choose to react positively or negatively. If you react negatively, you are pressing negative numbers, so you begin to think negatively and use negative words when speaking with others and yourself. You probably make statements that include the word 'not,' such as, "I cannot," "I cannot do it," "I do not feel like it," 'I cannot become as good as others" and "I am not talented." The sound of these sentences reminds me of a crying child calling out for a parent to help him overcome his difficulties because he cannot handle them by himself. The word 'not,' just as 'no', denies your possibilities, and when you use it to talk or formulate our thoughts, it's a bit like your mind becomes surrounded by high walls from which it can never escape.

Here's something else you should notice: when you pronounce the word 'no,' your muscles tighten and you prepare for mental or physical rejection; conversely, when you pronounce the word 'yes,' you relax and prepare yourself for acceptance by lowering your defenses and opening your mind to new possibilities.

Alternatively, you could use sentences that sound like insults aimed at yourself, such as, "I am unable," "I am a failure," "I am a good-for-nothing," "I am unable," "I am lazy" or "I am a loser." These expressions sound a bit like a whining child who, feeling small and inadequate, tries to attract attention to be comforted by grown-ups. What he means is, "that's the way I am; I cannot do anything about it; however, you could comfort me." Now that you are an adult, if you are still resorting to similar statements, it means that you are trying to recreate situations from your childhood in order to receive comfort; although doing so may have worked when you were a child, it may not necessarily work now, resulting in more disappointment as you don't receive the attention you crave.

Other negative sentences include self-deception, that is to say sentences that diminish the importance of missed objectives. Here are some examples: "Other things are more important," "I don't live for this," "I prefer other things," "I prefer using my brain," "I enjoy living a comfortable life" and so on. As a child, you probably used these excuses to manipulate the reality that bothered you, such as, for example, when your friends showed you toys that you could not have, to which you responded by saying that you could not stand them so you wouldn't feel bad. Now that you are an adult, if you customarily lessen or amplify the importance of your objectives based on whether you succeed or fail (if I can do it, then it matters; if I cannot do it, then it does not matter), this means that you are deeply affected by insecurity, which keeps you from facing negative results and turning them into positive experiences. In fact, you are avoiding facing your problems and keeping yourself from growing as an individual by getting tangled in your own psychological web.

Lastly, although I could provide more examples, consider those sentences that include alibis: "I am in pain again," "I cannot push myself," "I could worsen the situation" and so on.

When you try to do something and you do not reach your desired goal, if you react negatively and resort to negative language, you inevitably set your brain up to provide negative responses and use arguments that are closed off to the possibility of improving or finding a solution. These conditions leave you only one choice: giving up. To help you change perspective, it could be useful for you to understand why these sentences and expressions recur so often in the way you speak or think...

Until the age of 9, Teo was a puny child. This was partly due to his build and partly because, as a child, he did not practice any sports. Every time Teo tried to run or wrestle, his mother scolded him telling him not to do things like that, not to sweat, run or compete with others because he was so frail, therefore he would injure himself. Teo's mother loved him, but she did not realize that her overprotective tendencies could only limit him. As Teo was

constantly told, "Don't do this because you are not strong enough," he could do nothing else but convince himself that this must be true. During a school physical, the Doctor noticed that Teo was not in good health, so he persuaded Teo's mother to sign up the boy for swim courses at the local pool. Teo began to swim. Course after course, he developed a passion for swimming; he put his heart into it and he had no trouble making it into the swim team. However, his performance at swim meets was always disappointing. This was due to the fact that every time Teo approached the starting block, a strange sense of unrest took over him, halting his mind and muscles. A moment before diving, he was strong and full of energy; a moment later everything changed and he turned into a weak, fragile and incompetent child. Despite his passion for this sport, Teo took the sad decision to quit competitive swimming at the age of 15, as he realized that he had serious difficulties reaching his goals. His mother, always ready to keep him under her protective wing, consoled him by saying, "It's not your fault; I always knew that you were not strong enough."

A few years later, Teo returned to swimming. He did so because he felt the need to relax after spending days on the books to prepare for college finals, and swimming made him feel better. As he began frequenting the swimming pool, he noticed that they had part-time openings for lifeguards and a few hours of work allowed him to earn enough money to pay for books and entertainment. One day, one of his co-workers saw him swim. Impressed by how Teo glided through the water, he invited Teo to join the company's Masters swimming team. He explained to Teo what type of commitment this would require: three competitions a year, all in the good spirit of sport and friendship. At first Teo came up with a few excuses; then, as his co-worker insisted, Teo accepted. Teo found that the Masters swimming team was a wholesome, pleasant and laid-back environment, even though at practice everyone worked as hard as professionals. For Teo, Masters level exercises were not tough. His polished technique allowed him to use little energy to keep up with the team's fastest swimmers and for this reason he enjoyed continuing to swim with them, instead of going back to working out alone. It would be a perfect picture if this team came with no meets...

On the day of his first Masters competition, Teo's teammates were excited and they made bets on Teo's finals time for the fifty meter butterfly. On the other hand, Teo felt very unsettled; his worries and old fears made him feel weak and inadequate. Sounding like a broken record, his mind kept saying, over and over, "You are not strong enough." Teo dove in. As he swam, he slapped the water instead of capturing it gently. He was uncoordinated, inefficient and incredibly slow. His friends were floored; they couldn't believe their own eyes. At the end of the meet, his finals time was not only the last of the heat, but also worse than some of his teammates'.

Yet Teo succeeded because he had reached in true objective. His performance was once again in line with what his mother had always told him. And that was, in the end, that he was not strong enough.

When something happens to you and you resort to negative words and thoughts to face or retell the outcome to yourself or others, the consequences will be nothing short of disaster. On the other hand, if you use positive language, the outcome will change dramatically. I'll tell you what happened to me...

A while back, I spent much time practicing to improve my backstroke technique, mainly focusing on my turns. The most complicated moment for me was the part that came after the 'flip-turn,' when, for a few moments, I found myself belly-up below water level. In this position, I could not help but inhale pool water! I unwillingly experienced this bothersome outcome over fifty percent of the times. Well, if I reacted negatively to this situation, I would have probably told myself things like: "It cannot be done," "I am not good enough," "Backstroke is not for me," "This is a dumb stroke" or "Nobody ever explained how to do it and, until someone helps me, I will never succeed." Alternatively, I could have asked myself, "Why in the heck can't I do it?" As I mentioned earlier, your brain is like a calculator that gives results based on data received and life experiences. Faced with a similar question, my brain would have answered, "If you can't do it, then you are lacking" and this confirms the fact that "You should quit." Maybe at the beginning I would have pressed forward, not only to seek a solution to my problems, but also to reinforce my conviction that giving up was the best thing to do. I would have continued doing the same thing and obtaining exactly the same results. Conversely, wise men say, "It is insane to keep doing the same things and hoping to obtain a different outcome." In fact, I would have continued to fail repeatedly until I finally made the sad decision to quit the challenge.

How did things really go? I reacted in a positive way, asking myself a very simple question: "What am I doing wrong? How can I become aware of my mistakes so that I can find the solution?" Faced with this situation, I gave my mind a problem to solve and I devoted all my energy to solving it, knowing fully well that: "Doing the turn this way leads to my drinking pool water and getting tired;

there must be another way and, in order for me to find out what the right way is, I must gather more information." First of all, I repeated the exercise and I laid belly up about twenty times, not because I like hurting myself, but rather to gain a deep understanding of where my error lied. Then, I stood at the edge of the pool for approximately ten minutes watching others swim to uncover their secrets and techniques and observing two winning techniques: one way is to vigorously blow an excessive amount of air through your nose, and another way is to use your upper lip to help close your nostrils, simply by lifting your lips as if you were grimacing. After trying both techniques, I found that the second one was the one that worked best for me. Now when I lay down on my back below water level, I no longer have any issues!

Reacting positively or negatively is something that does not depend on a non-modifiable aspect of a person, her so-called character, but rather it begins from a personal decision. Granted, once you get used to reacting negatively, it begins feeling very natural for you until it becomes a habit, albeit a negative one. It is a bit like those who want to quit smoking: they know it's bad for them, but giving it up seems impossible. However, many before them have successfully quit.

Those who decide that they cannot change choose to live within their small boundaries: a place that they know well, which gives them limited reach. Those who decide to change leave their comfort zone and wander in search of new things to learn. When faced with a problem, you have a choice: you can continue to react like you have always done and use the tools in your confined reach to climb the mountain before you, or you can try to avoid closing yourself off to the world, leave your comfort zone and go discover other winning

ANTONIO LOGLISCI

techniques that others have successfully used before you.

When you succeed in reacting positively in front of what happens to you, then and only then you will be reaching out to the Adult inside you, that rational aspect of your personality that pushes you to find solutions that help you reach new limits, rather than crying or activating strategies to comfort you for your losses.

EMOTION
Winners and losers

When faced with a problem, some people react to solve and overcome their problem because they see it as a life challenge. Conversely, others stop and curse, feeling like destiny has yet again unleashed against them.

When making mistakes, some people react by trying to understand what has happened to them because they want to avoid making the same mistake in the future; so they experience growth and improvement, day after day. On the other hand, others look for someone to blame for what happened to them so they don't have to change the way they do anything, and things can always remain as they are.

There are people who lose a challenge and then rise above it. Conversely, others cannot find it in them to lift themselves up, so they just lay there, feeling sorry for themselves and hoping that, sooner or later, someone will come by to help them up. The former have winning reactions. The latter have losing reactions.

Sometimes, you may have belonged to the first group. Other times, you may have felt like you belonged to the second group. To feel like you belong here and there is absolutely normal, but be careful: those who can react positively more frequently live better lives; they are happier and they too become winners. Those who can't react positively become more easily tempted to react negatively, therefore they become losers.

The good news is that nothing remains the same and everything can be changed. The bad news is that, before you can begin to turn things around, you must awake from the deep slumber of losers and get moving by putting forth an effort in everything you do.

How can you tell whether you are sleeping or not? Below is a brief exercise, which, in its simplicity, may trigger a series of thoughts, known as reflection.

EXERCISE

**How would you react in the following situation?
Answer by quickly selecting one of the following responses.**

You are walking through a town with which you are not' familiar. You are headed to a club for a very important meeting. You are late. It's raining. You don't have an umbrella. You can't find your way. What would you say?
1. It's just my luck.
2. Did it have to rain today?
3. Did we have to meet here?
4. What excuse should I mention to justify my being late?
5. I should ask for directions, so I can avoid arriving even later. Oh well, these things happen. Next time I will consult the weather forecast and map my route on the Internet before I leave the house.

Solution

Regardless of the response you picked, consider one thing: the situation is what it is; there are no alternatives and you cannot rewind the present to go back and change your actions. At that moment in time, things are what they are. If you complain, stomp your feet or get angry, you will only stress yourself out and make things worse, running the risk that you may worsen the situation for yourself and for the people around you. Try a different approach. Try asking yourself what you could do next time to avoid ending up in the same situation.

CHAPTER 6: THE MASTERS SWIM TEAM

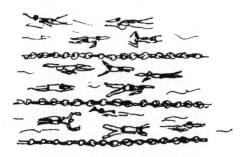

EXPERIENCE - Year zero

"In 1934, the Cozzi swimming pool was inaugurated in Milan. At the time, it was Europe's largest swimming pool and Italy's first indoor pool. In line with the standards of the time, its lane length was 33.33 meters. After so many years, and despite the fact that the Olympic lane size has since transitioned to 50 meters, nowadays the Cozzi pool still plays an important role in Milan's swimming scene. Granted, over the years, various other 25-meter and some 50-meter pools (Mecenate and Saini) were built, as well; however, no other major Swim Center worthy of the city's worldwide reputation has been built since 1934..."

When you try to use the Internet to get something done, most of the time you end up reading unsolicited data. Sometimes this unexpected information is enriching: it broadens your perspectives and leads you to do something better than how you had envisioned. However, in most cases, unsolicited data is distracting and using it only results in a waste of time. In recent days, I had been using the Internet to find a new swimming pool, but the sites I landed on were of little use. I was ready to throw in the towel, resigned to the idea that I would have to use the more convenient facility, despite the fact that it did not fully meet my expectations. But providence miraculously stepped in. On a Saturday afternoon, I was strolling through my neighborhood. Along the way I ran into a couple of guys who looked familiar. We looked at each other and smiled. I was pleasantly surprised to meet these guys, as I remembered that they belonged to the lost-long group of swimmers from last year. I asked them what had happened to them, and they told me that they had begun training in a nearby private facility, which offered competitive masters swimming. I was happy to have run into them and I was sure that I would join them; however, experience taught me that before signing up for anything, I should collect additional data. I didn't want to repeat the mistake I had made two years earlier, when, due to a care-free choice, I had signed up for a course that was too advanced for my abilities. I voiced my hesitation and the guys suggested that I participate in the pre-season meeting held by the facility's owners to introduce themselves to athletes in terms of management and annual objectives.

About a dozen people showed up for the meeting. I felt extremely happy to reconnect with familiar people, who greeted me with affection and reminded me of the good old days when, following one of coach Poncherello's workouts, they saw me laid up on a bench, elevating my legs. When the sports director arrived, the atmosphere remained relaxed, although silence gave the situation a certain air of importance. After the customary greetings, the speakers described the competitive nature of the Masters swimming team and stated that all its swimmers, as members of the Italian Swimming Federation (FIN) Masters division, were required to participate in the swim meets. The weekly commitment included three practices: one 1-hour and two 1.5-hour sessions. The coach, a single individual for the entire team, would prepare the training schedule according to a specific plan that would culminate in three periods of peak performance, coinciding with select meets. Participation in other weekly events (approximately once a week) was elective. Throughout the year, physical tests would be held to measure the athletes' performance level; and those willing to devote more time to training would have access to the pool on Sunday mornings for additional individual practice.

I listened intently, waiting for the catch. A couple of people, citing last year's experience, complained about the excessive strain of the workouts, especially considering that, once a week, practice would be held on consecutive days. The others and I, for my own good, supported these isolated voices with unveiled enthusiasm. As for me, I had never swum non-stop for one and one-half hours and I had never practiced three days a week; in fact, the only competition in which I had ever participated was a celebration rather than a true swim meet. However, I felt tempted by what had become a new and compelling challenge. I was just concerned about my current physical state. For a one and one-half month, I had been suffering from a stiff neck that did not seem to want to go away, despite taking medicine and doing physical therapy. I will never forget the day on which this my neck pain began...

It happened on the last day of July, just one day before summer vacation. I couldn't wait to leave the city: Milan's summer temperatures had become unbearable. Fortunately

we had an efficient air conditioning system at the office. Unfortunately, our room temperature setting was controlled by my co-worker, an overweight guy addicted to spiked coffee. His addiction resulted in the office thermostat being set to Alaskan temperatures, while we were exposed to African temperatures every time we went outside. The extreme temperature changes I was exposed to during my lunch breaks should be listed as "no-nos" in all medical self-help books. In fact, after being exposed to several extreme transitions from hot to cold weather, the muscles between my shoulder blades began to shiver a little, feeling a bit like an electric shock. This was only a temporary ailment, just a twitch.

However, a few hours later, when I left the office and went to take the subway, I felt my muscles twitching again, harder this time. I realized that, following this second twitching episode, my neck felt slightly stiff. I tried rotating my head to loosen up my neck muscles, but, as an overall sense of tightness came over me, I thought up a unique solution: "A good swim will fix it." And so I went to the swimming pool swam eighty laps and, the next day, I received my punishment...

"Am I awake? Yes, I am awake. My eyes are wide open, so I must be awake. But why can't I move? I must again be dreaming that nightmare in which I think I am awake, but I can't move! But I am sure that I am not dreaming. Well, then, why can't I get up? Come on little muscles, contract... on three: one, two and... three!" I felt pain, loads of pain, excruciating pain. In fact, I was screaming in pain. As I was still sitting in bed, I realized that I could not rotate my head without turning my entire body. What a nice way to begin my vacation!

Although I spent the entire summer receiving

myorelaxing injections and doing stretching exercises, by September my muscles were still not back to normal. My neck was now moving again, but my trapezium continued to hurt. I still intended to sign up for the new swim course; however, I was unsure whether I should skip the first few practices or just take it easy. I decided that I would begin right away, pairing up practice with some sports massages in the hope that this may accelerate my healing.

On my first swim practice, I swam as relaxed as a sloth, almost as if I was swimming on my own. I was in no condition to perform the workout, so I didn't really feel its impact. The others were swimming back and forth like lightning, but I felt like I would keep up with those in my lane. The exercises we performed reminded me of those imposed by our former coach Poncherello.

After a few weeks of taking it easy and with my muscles finally relaxing, I took courage and began turning it up a notch. It was at this point that I realized I had made a serious calculation error: the other swimmers were fast and I could not keep up with them, not even half the time! The practices were frenetic and we had no breaks: we had to swim twenty laps to warm up and cool down; then 50 meters ten times, 100 meters eight times, 200 meters four times and 400 meters once. Then, we had to restart from the beginning. Then pause for fifteen, twenty and twenty-five seconds. My goodness, I was so confused!!! What the heck was the instructor saying? He sounded like he had swallowed his math book! To keep from making a mistake, I watch the others and did as they do, or at least I tried, considering that things were truly chaotic: the water looked like it was on fire and confusion was the name of the game. Some swam slowly while others were very fast. The swimmers in the next lane zoomed by making me feel like a snail. The swimmers in my lane were either busy passing me or trying not be passed at all costs.

As if that weren't enough, I, like clockwork, alternated scratching my arms against the lane divider, drinking chlorine water and making major errors, as I wondered, "Who am I? Where am I? What am I doing?" At times, the frenzy spun so fast that my uneasiness began to feel like it was about to turn into panic. In my head, I kept screaming that it was time to stop. At the end of each practice, I felt like a survivor. My only comfort consisted in knowing that I was not the only one. A couple of girls were struggling as much as I was.

After a few hard weeks, we faced our first physical test of the season. I was told that all I had to do was swim eighty laps (2 kilometers) without ever stopping. I acted like I didn't understand. Last year's Cooper test had been enough to realize that these kinds of things were not meant for me. Plus, I thought that, generally speaking, swimming eighty consecutive laps was definitely not a good idea. Unfortunately for me, I could not back out. I asked myself if this would be the last thing that I would do in this course. There was nothing left for me to do but drag my heavy heart to that lane to find out...

"I am ready. I can do it. In the end, how hard can it be? Don't rush. Go slowly. Take it one lap at a time. I just need to get it done. It's just my first time. Come on, who cares if it's not perfect?!" My internal monologue was essential at stressful times like this. I needed it to reassure my inner child and tell him not to be afraid or scared because there was nothing to fear. I also tried to make myself feel at ease in the presence of the two other swimmers in my lane. "They are doing their own thing. Your pace should be your only reference point."

It was time to get started. The coach blew the whistle. I dove in, took off and I immediately asked myself, "What if I lose count of my laps? That's impossible. All I have to do is constantly repeat the current lap number. Lap one, one, one, one, one, one... two, two, two... three, three, three, three... four or was it five? It must be lap four; the return lap is always an even number. Now, did I say five or seven?!?" After less than ten laps, I lost count. I decided to round up; the coach would stop me if he saw me swimming too many laps.

Lap twenty. How did I do? Heat was the factor that bothered me the most. Then I had to deal with my breathing heavily, but I could bear it as long as it didn't involve any spleen pain. I was thinking clearly at the time: I could tell the black line from the rest of the pool. Thus far, there were no mermaids in sight.

Lap thirty. I could now read the writing at the bottom of the swimming pool. It said, "You will never make it!" My muscles felt heavy, and I was in pain. I almost had the feeling that somebody was lying on top on me. A big guy!

Lap forty. I was in a trance. I felt so numb that I did not even feel nervous about just being half way there.

Lap fifty. The other two swimmers were doubling me three times as quickly now. At every turn I looked up to obtain some sort of encouragement from my coach, but he was too busy noting times and laps to notice my need for encouragement. A mermaid invited me to follow her. So I did.

Lap sixty. One after another, the other two (twenty laps ahead of me) finished the test, leaving me to face my destiny alone. The good news is that my muscles were no longer burning; the bad news is that they were no longer contracting, either. My arms had become rows and I was just slapping them on the water.

Lap sixty-five. I began to see the light at the end of the tunnel and believing that I could make it. The number of laps was so high that I began feeling like a brute. The problem was that I was almost sitting still. I felt like it took me hours to complete one lap.

Lap seventy. I looked at my instructor with puppy eyes. Next to him there were guys laughing. It almost looked like somebody was saying, "Please, somebody shoot him down... he looks so hopeless!"

Lap seventy-nine. Incredibly, I am almost done. There is nothing left for me to do but lie still and motion-less, and wait for the current to make me float to the edge.

Lap eighty! Against all odds and the forecasts of my coach and fellow swimmers, I unexpectedly completed my eighty laps without stopping, an achievement that had seemed against all natural laws! They grabbed me by the arms and pulled me out of the pool, as I laid there looking like an exhausted castaway. Somebody laughed and somebody else said, "At one point we thought that you would give up... you were standing still!" That's right; standing still. I also felt like, at one point, what was moving was not me, but the lap below me. My final verdict: 2 kilometers in 43 minutes. I had no point of reference to know better, but one thing was for sure: I felt very good and I was proud of myself!

In addition to testing our fitness level (we would have to do it again in a few months), the purpose of this test was to infer the parameter with which the so-called "threshold pace" would be calculated. Here's my best understanding of this: during practice, when I had to repeatedly swim the same distances (50, 100, 200 and 400 meters), I must maintain my threshold pace for each distance and doing so would increase my aerobic strength. This was the theory, because in practice this translated into an unbearable effort, during which I could not even swim at the required pace the first time.

I noticed a substantial change in my physical condition. My fainting episodes were almost completely gone; to make up for it, I began getting cramps. It happened almost regularly: after an hour of swimming, my leg muscles began to struggle. The most recurring sensation was feeling like a knife cut through my calves. When this happened, I could always manage by myself: I turned on my hazards, parked in the emergency lane and waited for the pain to go away. One time, it happened only once, I got cramps in both my quads at the same time. I panicked and felt like I couldn't reach the edge of the pool. With tremendous effort, I grabbed the wall and rolled out of the pool. My coach and the lifeguard grabbed my feet to help stretch out my muscles. The scene looked like the final match of a soccer tournament, when, before going into overtime, the soccer players lay down on the ground to get their legs massaged. The problem is that, as soon as my rescuers let go of my feet, my calves began violently contracting again. It took five endless minutes to resolve the situation; then I limped my way to the locker room. The coach pointed out that, although I may not realize it, swimming makes you lose fluids and minerals, and therefore it would be a good idea to drink water during the workout. So I brought water. As if to signal my presence, from that day forward, every time I have swum, there has always been a canteen at the edge of the swimming pool. Our first swim meet was held in December at the Gnecchi Memorial in Bergamo. My coach asked me to pick two events to swim. I looked through the list of events searching for the shortest distances. I found the 50 meter freestyle, but I had to pair it up with the 100 meter breaststroke...

Sunday morning; Bergamo city pool. The lobby was full of people of every age. Some are in warm-ups, while others are wondering around the sales stands in their robes. In the back of the room, there was a line of people waiting by the front desk. One of my fellow swimmers noticed my puzzled look and explained that those people were in line to pick up meet sheets and competition kits. When I arrived in the locker room I noticed that the others were randomly changing everywhere. There weren't many changing rooms so, instead of waiting, one could change while standing here and there, a somewhat precarious and ridiculous balancing act, which, judging from everyone's indifference, wasn't very unusual.

The atmosphere was relaxed as people were cracking jokes. From time to time, there were moments of tension for the upcoming meet, but the feeling was far from exasperation. I was amused as I looked around because this was my debut and I had no expectations; I felt free to explore my surroundings like a child taken to a new place.

Donning my bathing suit, robe and deck shoes, and carrying my swim bag weighed down by my clothes and coat, I joined the rest of the team on the stands, being careful not to slip on the wet and very slippery floor. I joined my teammates and I noticed that most people looked sleepy, while others looked a bit tense and anxious. Our coach, ever in the know, suggested we swim a few laps before the beginning of the meet. I looked at the water somewhat reluctantly because the idea of being immersed in water on a cold December morning was as inviting as a trip to the dentist. As usual, my sense of duty overruled my wishes, so I dove into what could easily be mistaken for rows of fishing nets.

The taste of chlorine made me feel sick. I fought back, controlled my reaction and began swimming. The guy ahead of me was very slow, while the guy behind me wouldn't stop scratching my feet. When I arrived at the wall, I stood in a line of people and waited in line to do my flip-turn. When there are so many people around you, the unspoken truth is that if you do not get kicked, then you're the one who must be doing the kicking. I started swimming again. I swam a couple of laps without taking a break; then I had to stop once again to wait for the slower swimmers. I took the important decision of interrupting my warm-up as I was sure that this would have no impact on the final result. I dried myself off and began chatting cheerfully with all those who were willing to do so although they may be in a potentially stressful situation.

After spending an hour watching the performance of others, there came the much-anticipated time for me to swim the 100 meters breaststroke. The thought that just a few years earlier I could not even swim this stroke made me smile. I headed toward the pool area where the event organizers, armed with bullhorns, marshaled the participants to join their heats. As usual, my last name was mispronounced, and, as usual, I responded with a smile, over-looking the mistake. I joined the other swimmers in my heat: three guys in their sixties, two ladies in their forties and two others who looked like they were the same age as me. One of my peers was a girl, who was competing for the first time; she confessed that she was utterly terrorized by what was about to happen. I was curious, so I asked, "What are you specifically afraid of?" She looked taken aback; then she began to laugh.

Within a few minutes spent laughing at each other's jokes, we found ourselves in front of the diving blocks. Compared to the previous year's meet at the Cozzi pool, this competition felt more official and rigorous. There was a line judge positioned next to each block. There was a huge electronic scoreboard that displayed each athlete's times. There were chairs laid out for athletes to leave their clothes. They even had a speaker that announced the upcoming swimmer's names.

And the start procedure was terribly serious. The coach explained that, as soon as I heard the words, "take your mark," I must freeze on the block until the beep allowed me to proceed. Any movement would cause me to get disqualified for a false start. "No problem," I replied; I won't move until I see the others dive! I checked my goggles one more time, realizing that I could not make them tighter than they already were, unless I wanted to take a trip to the hospital, which was located next to the pool. Here we go; the start sequence began with the head judge blowing the first long whistle. I quickly visualized what I had to do: four laps of breaststroke... easy. I climbed on the block. As the judge said, "On your mark," I bent over my starting block and froze. At the electronic beep, I dove into the water through a slightly unclean dive and thus began my very first FIN-sanctioned competition. The first lap was rather uneventful. The second lap was a bit more laborious. The third lap was decidedly harder. The fourth lap felt like it would never end. However, I touched the wall and finished the race without feeling worn out. I pulled up on the wall to see my time on the electronic scoreboard, but the athletes preparing for the following heat obstructed my view. Anyway, I received that information through the loudspeaker: "Athlete Antonio Loglisci was disqualified due to irregular flip turn." Well done, Antonio. This adventure in masters swimming could not have started any better! I went to see my coach to understand what happened because it looked to me like I had done everything by the rules. The coach had heard the disqualification announcement and watched my swim, so he explained that I had touched the wall with only one hand instead of two. One hand? Turns? Right, I completely forgot to pay attention to all that. I laughed at the situation because, honestly, I had a lot of fun. My coach said that, before getting disqualified, my time was around one minute and forty-six seconds.

An hour later, I was up for my next event: the 50 meter freestyle. I was always ready for this event; however, my only relentless doubt was figuring out which type of turn I should use: should I take a chance and use the quick and efficient flip turn or should I just touch the wall and turn around? In training, I could never do a flip-turn correctly because the temporary lack of oxygen caused me breathing troubles. I wrapped up my thoughts and decided to just let my instincts take over; it went something like, "When that time comes, I will do whatever I feel like doing."

As our heat lined up, I realized that one of my teammates was next to me. This was surprising because during practice he was stronger and more resilient than me. Moments later, I found myself standing on the starting blocks and ready to take on the water with all the strength I had in my arms. At the start, I took off like a rocket, but I saw that my teammate was one meter ahead of me. At the turn, I completed the fastest flip-turn of my life, and I have no idea how I did it. At this point I could no longer see my teammate! I swam like crazy and I quit breathing. At the end of the swim, I touched the wall before him. This time I could clearly see the scoreboard and nothing or nobody announced that I was disqualified. In fact, everyone was quite impressed by the displayed time of 32"88 for my first freestyle competition. I did not know what to say, as I didn't have a reference point to gauge my performance. One thing was for sure: I felt like I was flying!

A few weeks after my first competition in Bergamo, the newness worn off as I began feeling overwhelmed by the ever-growing, challenging workouts dished out by our coach. Going to the pool three times a week did not help much because every time I got ready to enter the water, I felt a strange sense of anxiety taking over me with endless limiting questions, such as, "Will I make it through practice without getting cramps? Will I be able to complete a good share of the exercises? Will I get sick? Before practice, my state of mind was that of someone who had been tasked with unloading a truck of refrigerators and, at the end of each practice session, my body sent me disapproving signals on how it felt abused. I often wondered why I was subjecting myself to such torture: in the end, nobody was ordering me to be there; in fact, I could easily attend a less challenging course. The answer was always the same: there was something I enjoyed in all this tormenting.

Months went by and I continued practicing and going to meets. I progressively found myself in new heats, but I never again had the chance to compete against a fellow team member. I realized that it was difficult to give it my all when I had no point of reference, so I just competed for the fun of it, without a set objective or specific motivation. The standings for my group, in which I was far from the top, made me feel increasingly uneasy in competition. It felt like the whole thing was a pretty useless endeavor. I continued to tell myself that I would never win anything or go anywhere, so I couldn't understand why I was doing all this. As this was my state of mind, I was disqualified two more times for false starts and overall achieved meaningless results. In the Lombardy Regional Masters Swimming Championships, my 50 meter breaststroke time lingered around 45″, while, during a meet in a 50-meter pool in Brescia, I realized how it was so much better to swim in smaller pools. The Varedo Trophy meet, held in a 50-meter pool toward the end of the season, brought on my next intense emotion...

The weather was nice so my teammates and I were lying out in the sun, while hanging out in the yard outside the swimming pool. Unlike other master swimmers, who were indoors and preparing for their event, we were relaxing and we could care less about the outcome of the meet. For a sense of respect, we took turns looking into the pool area to see what event was on. When it was my turn to go check on the events, I saw that the 200 individual medley was about to get underway. There was still time; I could go back outside, but something told me to stay and watch that event, which involved swimming 50 meters butterfly, 50 meters backstroke, 50 meters breaststroke and 50 meters freestyle. Just the thought of it made me tired! I stood there in awe as I watched those athletes swim. They were very powerful and extremely strong, although the pool water seemed to slow them down and tire them quite a bit. Their arm strokes were always powerful, bold and never feeble. During the breaststroke events, every time the swimmers emerged to breathe, it almost sounded like they were roaring. It seemed like I was watching an exhibition of aliens, not humans. How in the heck can anyone have so much energy while swimming at that speed?!? Then I thought of how nice it would be to know how to do something like that. If I had only made an effort to learn how to swim when I was a child...

One-half hour later, it was my turn to swim 50 meters breaststroke: only one long lap to swim at maximum speed. Once again, my heat comprised the usual widely representative group: some elderly ladies, one guy who was about my age and many girls. One of these girls looked familiar. I took a better look, as she looked at me, too. I began to smile, while she was outright laughing. It was hard to tell who was more surprised to see the other in a swimming competition. That woman was my "old" swimming instructor, the one who saw me pass out on the day of my first swim lesson, and she could not begin to picture me participating in a swim meet. She kindly congratulated me. I thanked her, but on the inside I thought that it was time for me to test how much my swimming had improved. In the end, if we were in the same heat, it meant that our seed times were about the same; therefore I may have a chance at beating her. I know it's not very gentleman-like to chat with somebody while thinking of beating her, but deep down inside this was a coveted opportunity to show myself how far I had come from my first lesson.

Here we go. The head official blew the whistle and we climbed on the starting blocks. At the start signal, I leaped into the pool with all my strength so I could quickly gain an advantage. As I emerged from the dive, which I tried to stretch out as much as possible, I began swimming, pushing my stroke as much as possible. I did not turn around and I didn't try to see where my instructor was in reference to me, but out of the corner of my eye I saw that we were right next to each other. At the thirty-meter mark, I began feeling fatigue. My biceps and hand muscles burned like crazy, but I clenched my teeth and continued to turn my arms without stopping. The last few meters of my swim were a bit untidy; then, as I was just a few inches from the wall, I decided to stretch out that arm stroke to gain precious moments. After touching the wall, I turned around and realized that there was no need to do that: I finished way ahead of my former instructor. With a nice smile, she looked at me and said, "Congratulations. You did a really good job!"

I felt like I had reached a milestone and obtained definite proof that I had now transitioned to a higher level. Although it was still true that since joining the masters swim team I had always been the slowest swimmer, it was also true that at the beginning I could barely complete two laps without stopping. Being aware of that fact was to become my strength. I must never forget where I came from and what I achieved thanks to my will to succeed.

ANALYSIS - Motivation 101

When your challenges get tougher, how do you find the strength to carry on? When all you feel is pain, what do you rely on to react? When fatigue has claimed all your energy, how do you clench your teeth and unleash your final attack?

San Alfonso del Mar is a Chilean resort well-known around the world for its natural swimming pool, which was featured in the Guinness Book of Records. The lap length is more than one kilometer long and, in some spots, the natural pool reaches depths of 35 meters, holding 250 million liters of saltwater. Therefore, this allows pool users to practice various aquatic sports, such as windsurfing, sailing and kayaking. The perimeter of the pool is dotted with hotel facilities of every kind, making of this place an authentic heaven for tourist.

On December 19, 2008, Mauro Giaconia went to San Alfonso del Mar not for vacation, or maybe not primarily for that, but to try to make history by swimming more kilometers in twenty-four hours than anyone in human history. Mauro was not the last kid on the block; he was not an improvised extreme swimmer just attempting to be

included in the Guinness Book of World Records. In fact, for years Mauro had been specifically training to perform various extraordinary swims. His many achievements included an individual crossing from Ustica to Mondello (70 km in open sea), a tenfold crossing of the Strait of Messina (he still holds the World Record for this one), the crossing of the Strait of Gibraltar and countless swimming pool marathons of six, eight and even twenty-four hours. Mauro was trained and prepared, but obviously he was not sure of the outcome.

To help guide his trajectory, Mauro had some floats set up in order to create a circuit of 1200 meters that went through the most famous locales of the artificial lagoon. At 10:04 PM, Mauro entered the water wearing a wetsuit, swim cap and goggles, and he began swimming. The weather conditions were not favorable at all: the water temperature ranged from 20 to 22°C and the swimming pool was continuously swept by cold ocean breeze. Mauro's biggest challenge was the salt water and, as hours went by, his lips and mouth started cracking like dry earth. Despite all that, Mauro pressed on. Under the incredulous gaze of the numerous people that took turns watching him, he continued to swim non-stop for an entire day. From time to time, somebody looked out of his hotel room window to check that he hadn't quit. On the other hand, the next day at 10:04 PM, Mauro, with a dry mouth but in good physical conditions, triumphantly exited the swimming pool as he successfully set a new world record, swimming a total distance of one hundred and one kilometers.

One journalist asked him how such a thing was possible and Mauro replied, "When you think that your arms can't go on anymore, it's your head that keeps going."

MOTIVATION
=
VALUES x REINFORCEMENTS x OBJECTIVES

When you have a solid motivation, nothing can keep you from achieving the most incredible endeavors. But what exactly makes your motivation a solid one?

Three main factors:
- first of all, you need **values** to generate it;
- then you need **objectives** to stimulate it;
- lastly, you need **reinforcement** to support it.

To help you better understand what I mean, I will use my previous stories as examples.

My motivation to swim originated from a value that I hold very dear: my health. If I feel healthy, then I am considerably more apt to feeling happy. Conversely, when I am not healthy, my happiness decreases. After I took the physical administered by the company for which I worked, I felt like my health was at risk, and this took away a good share of my happiness. Now I had a reason to get moving, and this generated my motivation (regaining my health). Before I could complete the action to "go to the pool", I had to experience a spark, that is to say the negative emotion felt by looking at myself in the mirror of that clothing shop, where I gained visible proof that my health was beginning to deteriorate. My newly acquired awareness made me feel the urgency to do something, so my intentions finally turned into action and, within a few days, I signed up for my first swimming course, challenging my own natural dislike of water.

My motivation began working inside me, allowing me

not to care so much about embarrassing situations and to hang on tight in moments of physical weakness. I overcame the initial obstacles and I even began feeling good about the first positive signs, as I noticed small but significant improvements.

I gradually began increasing my number of laps and slowly began to lose weight: these were two immediate signs that my health was on the upswing, confirming that I was on my way to regaining happiness. As I increased the number of laps I swam, I found the energy to resist the physical suffering caused by this challenging sport. With growing energy, my ability to take on a higher number of laps increased, as well. This virtuous circle allowed me to reach the end of the first year with increased motivation, reinforced by my first positive results. So if everything works so well, why does effective motivation not last? In order for your motivation to become solid, you need two conditions.

First of all, you must know your values, those beliefs based on which you make meaningful choices in life. Identifying your values is no easy task: it requires analytical skills and an attentive analysis of your past experiences. I cannot tell you what your values are, but I can help you understand to what I am referring by explaining how my parents affected my choices. My primary values include health, freedom, growth and passion. As I said earlier, caring about my health pushed me to pursue a sport. Swimming worked like a charm because, as I could swim freely, it satisfied another one of my values: freedom. Last but not least, my passion for swimming increased more and more also because swimming allowed me to measure the continuous growth of my abilities and self-esteem.

The second condition that creates a solid motivation is your ability to produce reinforcements through the use of adult and positive reactions when facing things that happen to you. To understand what I mean, think of this: after my first tragic swim lesson, I succeeded in telling myself "good job" for the simple fact that it took courage for me to show up for the second lesson. Then, I told myself "good job" for not having passed out a second time. Next, I told myself "good job" for having advanced to the next level. After that, I congratulated myself for properly learning the breaststroke basics. Finally, I prided myself in completing my first thirty-six laps and so on.

If you react positively when facing what happens to you and you make an effort to identify how you can grow from your experiences, you will automatically advance; if you cannot do that, then you are predisposed to give up on your challenges because, if you don't accumulate positivity, it means that you are taking home negativity, and when you are loaded with enough failure, you feel like giving up.

As I already said, the ability to seize the positive aspect of what happens to you depends on your reactions, and you can change the way you react to things by tapping into positive language when you speak with others and, most of all, when you speak with yourself. Don't forget that feeling "good" depends entirely on you. If, for example, when you take swim lessons, nobody ever says, "Good job," maybe because your instructor likes keeping things a bit too cool, then it should be up to you to mark your own results. Only by doing so you can fuel up with the energy you need to strengthen and support your motivation.

Objectives, together with values and reinforcements, represent another major factor in motivation because they drive you to act. Acting without an objective is a bit like driving a car without knowing where you are going. It can be fun at first, but over the long run things may get dull. As I worked on defining my objectives, I found it convenient to arrange them on three levels: daily, medium-term and long-term objectives. Let me give you some examples...

- During my early swim lessons, my daily objective was that of resisting until the end of the lesson, without passing out or getting sick; the medium-term objective was to swim an increased number of laps and to swim a bit better; and the long-term objective was to lose weight and learn to swim well.
- In the masters swimming courses, my daily objective was to keep up and skipping as few exercises as possible; my medium-term objective was to get better test results; and my long-term objective was to become increasingly more fit and improving my time in my favorite events (50 meter freestyle and 50 meter breaststroke).
- Today, after many years of swimming in the masters league, my daily objective is to perfect my technique while keeping up with my repetition intervals; my medium-term objective is to improve my competition times and the way I feel about them; and my long-term objective is to set new personal records, make new experiences and maintain a clean bill of health.

When you set your objectives, it is vitally important to commit them to writing because only in this way they become a precise commitment to yourself. I suggest you annotate all your results because, in a few years, you will be able to look back and admire the improvements that you have made. I wrote down many things: the number of laps completed at the end of my swim first course, the year in which I completed my first kilometer of swimming, as well as my times in practice and meets. To keep my notes organized, I created some spreadsheets using a simple software program. Today, these spreadsheets have become an interesting database as they contain specific records (i.e. long-distance pool and short-distance pool) of meets I participated in, times I obtained, significant achievements, test results and, obviously, medium- and long-term objectives. I tried keeping track of my time sheets for every single workout assigned by my coach; then I decided to limit my recording efforts to a simple estimate of the kilometers swum over an entire season.

Writing objectives and recording data is how you determine a "quality" work because, if you don't write down what you wish for and what you have achieved, you will not be able to objectively grasp how you did it and, consequently, what you need to focus on to improve. By doing so, you can also avoid psychological dynamics commonly observed in losers, which consist of stating an objective only after having achieved it for fear that others may gather the loser's inability to accept failure. Remember: if you don't put forth an honest and sincere effort, over the long run you will lose interest in what you are doing. This is also true when you don't define precise objectives. But how does one create a precise objective? Simply use SMART objectives. There are various definitions of SMART objectives. Below, you will find my favorite one....

S stands for specific: an object must be identifiable and non-mistakable. Here's an example of a specific objective: to go from 20 to 18 arm strokes to complete a lap. An example of a non-specific objective is: improving your freestyle (this sounds more like a wish).

M stands for measurable: in order to state whether you

achieved your objective or not, you must establish a way to measure it. Here's a correct example: improved breaststroke technique means that you can complete a single lap with only 8 cycles of arm strokes. An incorrect example would be: technical improvement happens when you feel like you are swimming faster.

A stands for ambitious: your objective must require effort, otherwise it would feel like scoring into an empty soccer goal. In terms of objectives, if you establish something that can be achieved easily, then you are not defining a goal, but just a point of passage. An example of an ambitious objective is to swim 8 laps of butterfly, starting from being able to swim only 4 laps. An example of a not so ambitious objective would be to swim 100 laps of butterfly starting from being able to swim 96 laps.

R stands for reachable: your objective must be realistic and it must aim at something that is within your possibilities. If, as an objective, you say that you want to set a world record and you can't even swim two laps without running out of breath, it follows that you will face strong frustration. Here's an example of a realistic objective: reach three personal records over the course of the season. A not-very-realistic example would be: advancing to the Olympics after participating in masters swimming.

T stands for defined over time: your objective must have "a deadline," otherwise it serves no purpose. Here's a correct example: to swim the 100 meter butterfly within two years. A non-SMART example is: to compete in the 1500 meter freestyle, sooner or later.

My advice: set an objective for every single practice because motivation must be fueled daily. Treat your objective as a delicate plant and it will bloom beautifully. A similar approach would eliminate the possibility of saying, "tonight I don't feel like going swimming." It can happen that you go through periods of fatigue. However, as you may have noticed, some people seem to be affected by chronic laziness and they act surprised when somebody shows energy and a sense of initiative, even after spending years practicing four times a week. I have my way of doing things...

Every morning, when I wake up, I visualize the day ahead of me, "fast forwarding" the movie of my life. I stop fast-forwarding to observe the best moments, which I enjoy watching in slow motion. As I approach the final part of the day, I think of the time at which I will go swimming. At this point, I plan my goal for practice. Sometimes this consists of doing all the flip-turns properly, while other times I focus on performing a correct recovery by keeping my elbows high while swimming freestyle or keeping up to speed with the swimmer that precedes me, without letting him get too far ahead. These small daily objectives clearly define my swims, which, by becoming unique and different, allow me to have fun always and no matter what.

On the first year of masters swimming, I had no knowledge of all these things. The end result was that, within a few months, I completely lost myself in the whirlwind of swim meet events and I ended up being disqualified various times, obtaining random results. The only times in which I succeeded in focusing my energy and obtaining satisfactory performances were when I defined a precise objective, such as, for example, that of swimming faster than somebody I knew, who was in the same heat as me. This happened at the swim meet in Bergamo, when I swam in the same heat as my teammate, and in Varedo, when I swam against my former instructor. This happens because, when an objective is visible, it is easy to define and it allows you to focus on a specific target. In all other cases, even when I wanted to reach challenging results, I just went as far as wishing and hoping that it would happen, without taking any concrete steps to achieve my objective; however, when you leave things to chance, something good will also happen by chance.

Your objective must be precise and definable so that it may be visualized. This is another reason why your goals must be committed to writing; if you see them, then you can evaluate, analyze and understand to what degree they are SMART. Most of all, when you see them you can record them in your mind. Before winning eight gold medals at the Peking Olympics and leaving an indelible mark in swimming history, Michael Phelps used to post notes on his mirror showing the event times that he wanted to achieve in order to see them continuously.

Once visualized in your mind, an objective will allow you to focus all your energy on it, enabling you to reach extraordinary results.

EMOTION
It's not bad for you!

For those who, like me, entered the world of swimming through the service door and joined the 'dance party' not knowing how to dance, diving right into the action to prove that they too are part of the team may be a very hard thing to do. When you enter the water and believe that all you have to do is practice, you'll soon experience a whirlwind, internally and externally. "Warm up. Swim 500 meters, pick your stroke. Now do two series of these: 8 x 50 meters, 4 x 100 meters and 2 x 200 meters. Speed 80%." And that's already hard work. "Watch your arm, bend your elbow and stretch out." Goodness, there is so much to do. Somebody is touching my feet. What does he want from me?!? He is passing me. I must be swimming slowly... so I'll speed up. I can't take it anymore; my body is giving up on me. My heart feels like it's exploding and I am breathing heavily. My body is shot: it doesn't do what I tell it to do and it tires easily. I will never get better: I am not cut out for sports. But most of all... why am I doing this?

When you get in the water, you are sure that you can do it. Then, when you exit the water and believe that you have not achieved your goal, you feel like you'll never get better. At this point, your mind offers you two pills: the blue pill, which is easy to swallow and makes you forget everything so you can go back to being what you have always been; and the red pill, which is hard to swallow and makes you feel fatigue, but, little by little, even crawling on your elbows as if you were in a desert with no water to drink and you can't take it anymore, you slowly begin to pull yourself up. As if an evil snake was watching over you, every time you finish practice you are always faced with the same choice, until you make the final decision to take a massive dose of red pills. From that moment forward, all you have to endure becomes also fun, and then you'll finally grasp the meaning of the famous quote by movie character, boxer Rocky Balboa to his opponent Ivan Drago, "My mother hit me harder!" In fact, in the end, it doesn't hurt so much.

EXERCISE

Define 3 objectives, one daily, one medium-term and one long-term objective. Then fill out the blocks...

Select three objectives	Specify each objective	Give yourself a deadline	Did you reach your objective?	If not, why not?
1..........				
2..........				
3..........				
Example: number of laps completed in one hour of swimming	_100 laps in 40 minutes_	_By June_	_No._	_I could not attend every practice._
Example: Improve personal record for 100 freestyle	_Maximum time 1:05"_	_By May_	_Yes!_	

CHAPTER 7: OPEN WATERS

EXPERIENCE - New experiences

After a year of masters swimming, I realized that I was now a new person. Three intense practices a week definitely got me back in shape, making me reach, at the age of 32, a weight of 141 lbs. and size 34-36. Also considering the importance of muscle tone development, I can say that, from a physical point of view, I became an athlete. Even from the viewpoint of sports, things were going better. Despite the fact that my technique must be improved, I felt more confident, more powerful and more capable to face extended exertion. In my last 2-kilometer test, I had successfully improved my performance by four whole minutes, transitioning from forty-three minutes in October to thirty-nine the following May. But there was something about exercising in the water that made me feel decidedly at ease, going well beyond my good looks or physical shape: something called awareness of one's own means. I felt more in touch with my body; like I had better control over it and that I was reading its signals more leisurely. In fact, I felt like I had reached the best balance of body and mind that I had ever had.

At the beginning of my swimming adventure, the sole thought of being in the water upset all my senses. Excessive information received from my brain ("you are sinking," "you are tired," "you are drinking," "you can't breathe," "you are not moving") made me lose it, so I ignored my body's feedback on balance and I ended up frantically spinning arms and legs in random order. By now, I had learned to relax and calmly process the data received from the various parts of my body, which, instead of saying, "look, you're drowning; you're nothing but an idiot," sent precise alerts on the state of my floating, which progressively worsened as time went by and fatigue increased. This type of information was fundamental for me to manage my energy so that I could have continuous swim autonomy for at least one hour.

A more attentive analysis revealed that the most significant change took place in my heart: at first it was reluctant to dive into this sport, while now it was overflowing with immense passion for it. Some of the memories and negative emotions that I used to feel when I hated swimming now seemed so foreign to me; it almost felt like those feelings had never belonged to me. My love for swimming led me to constantly search new ways to enjoy this sport; in fact, one day I learned of some events that, instead of being held at the pool, took place in open waters. More specifically, during a meet held in May, I ran across a flier that advertised a water crossing, that is to say a swim open to amateurs, competitive swimmers and masters level swimmers, which involved crossing a lake from side to side.

I avidly read those lines; then I asked for additional information from people who had already participated in similar events. I gathered information on difficulty, pitfalls and winning strategies. As my head filled up with data, I was ever more convinced that swimming an open waters crossing would go a long way in terms of my experience in personal safety. Although increasing the distance I swam or my in-pool endurance made me feel like I was a good swimmer, succeeding in completing such a high visibility endeavor, which required no measurement to be appreciated, felt like a heroic feat. Among the various events available, I found one that I felt best matched my abilities by eliminating the longest crossing (Eremo crossing - 3.3 kilometers) and looking up those held by the tourism board of Orta San Giulio (by Lake Orta) and Mandello del Lario (Lake Lario), respectively measuring 1.4 and 1.5 kilometers. As a moment of hesitation took over me, I decided to sign up for the shorter crossings.

As days went by and the first crossing drew closer, my mind began experiencing strange visions and day-dreams. I almost always visualized pretty much the same thing: I found myself in the middle of a lake, all alone, and I had no idea which way to go as all directions appeared to be the wrong way. It took some time and a few reruns to understand the meaning of this strange message from the future à la Donnie Darko, which may be simply summarized in three words: "You are completely unprepared!"

Right, it's true; I was so wrapped up in finding an event that would fulfill my need to experience a crossing that I overlooked the fact that I had absolutely zero experience in open waters. Well, when I went to the beach in Romagna, I swam a few meters past the cliffs, where the water level drops from shallow to deep, but those swims never lasted more than a minute/one and one-half minute; then, as I feared that I would run out of energy, I headed right back to shore or toward the closest floating mattress around by simply telling its owner, "Will you allow me to rest for a minute? You see, I am cramping." My only certainty was that, by swimming three times a week for approximately three kilometers, I would develop twice the amount of energy needed for a crossing distance of 1.5 kilometers...

It was Sunday and a beautiful day in July. The sun was high in the sky and warming up our exposed skin. It felt nice. We were on the shore of Lake Orta, in a locality known as Pella. There were approximately three hundred people, all wearing bathing suits, and everyone was crammed on a small landing. Several of us repeatedly asked the event organizers where exactly we should land on the opposite shore. The answer we received was always the same, "There." Faced with a very confused crowd of people, they reassured us by saying that there would be some boats positioned along the course to show us the way. I smiled, as I pictured myself stopping in the middle of the lake and asking, "Excuse me, can you please tell me where the finish line is?" As I was afraid that something like that could happen to me, that day I had decided to wear my contacts, which I usually did not wear.

Another issue I had considered was how I would deal with the low water temperature. From the information gathered from Internet searches, I learned that low water temperatures could represent a serious problem. To stabilize body temperature, many experts suggest the use of lanolin, an animal fat that seems to have curiously insulating powers. It did not take long for me to track down some lanolin, although the pharmacist who sold it to me had a sinister smile when he delivered it.

The event was to start in twenty minutes. As I had read on the Internet, I proceeded to open the jar of lanolin to spread on my body. Almost as an instinct, I inhaled the smell of this substance. My mind went back a few years...

In my memory, I was about 8 years old. It was summer time. I was in the region of Apulia, in a small village in the countryside of the province of Bari, where my parents were born. My aunt was with me, holding my hand. She was smiling at me. I was happy. She was taking me to see her farm animals. I couldn't wait because I knew that I would soon get to touch rabbits and chickens. We reached a small wooden structure. Before opening the door, my aunt once again looked over at me; then she grabbed the handle and pulled the door back. My senses were faced with a tangled situation: total darkness, suffocating heat and a very unpleasant pungent smell. We approached the cages while walking on soft pavement covered with hay. We were surrounded by the deafening squealing of agitated animals. Once we arrived in front of the rabbit cage, my brain provided the answer I was waiting for: "...it is the most powerful smell of poop that you have ever smelled in your life!" I felt like I was going to faint!

All of a sudden, I re-opened my eyes and, moving quickly, I replaced the lid of the jar, thinking that, all in all, cold temperatures are not so hard to withstand. Then I thought twice and, for my own good, I decided to pinch my nose and spread lanolin over the most sensitive areas of my body: my abdomen, stomach, armpits and neck. I notice with pleasure that everyone around me moved away; the only ones who dared to stand with me are my two friends, as they too were partly covered in lanolin. After a few moments, once the damage was already done, the organizers announced that the water temperature, even in areas away from the shore, ranged around 25°C. How nice.

Five minutes following departure, my mind began to go over the text of the release form, which the event organizers made me sign when he delivered the participant's packet. Nothing major, except this one sentence: "...in case of death, the organizers shall not be held liable." Perplexity number one: liable to whom? Perplexity number two: do we run such a risk? Anxiety began to creep up, and I almost felt like I had just handed a blank check to a thief. To make me feel even more worried, my mind dwelled on the different treatment reserved to Masters level swimmers and Amateurs. The latter were issued a safety buoy to tie around their waist, so if they got tired, they could hold on to the buoy and rest. We masters swimmers were given a pat on the shoulder, as if to say, "C'mon, you don't really need one of those."

I grabbed all the negative thoughts that were spinning through my brain and I dragged them to my mental recycling bin. The drop in temperature was not shocking; in fact, I realized that, on that hot day, being immersed in water felt really well. I took a few arm strokes and I immediately found myself in deep water. I swam for approximately thirty meters and reached the start area reserved for Competitive swimmers. I was laughing inside, thinking that I had already swum thirty out of the required 1400 meters. After a few moments, the judge gave the start signal. At that time, something odd happened: everyone took off like a rocket, spinning their arms and legs as if they only had 100 meters to swim. I kept telling myself, "That's crazy. It is a long-distance event; why are they swimming so hard? What are they trying to prove? Where do they think they are going?" Within a few seconds, I found myself only surrounded by my thoughts and my snail pace. I didn't even have time to get accustomed to swim solo, that the front-runners of the amateur category caught up to me and, with a self-congratulatory smile, even visible below water level, passed me while carefully agitating their safety buoy. It seemed as if they all made faces at me so the joke would be complete. I didn't care, also because, in murky waters, my vision was limited and, within a few moments, they disappeared behind a cloud of bubbles. Here's a problem that I had not taken into consideration: I could not see a thing! My visibility was one, maybe two meters; then all I saw was just a yellow-green wall heated by the sun rays refracted by the water surface. In those conditions, it was difficult for me to gauge my speed. Plus, I found it impossible to figure out whether I was swimming in the right direction. So I wondered, "Should I stop for a moment? What if I don't regain my pace?"

After about ten minutes of non-stop questions, I quit hesitating and pulled my head out of the water while slowly swimming the breaststroke. I was barely treading water: for hundreds and hundreds of meters around me, I saw nothing but water. I was smack in the middle of the lake with no opportunity to set down a foot anywhere. My only small reassurance was the presence of a boat about one hundred yards away, which, even in case of need, would be impossible to reach. I quit thinking about that, took a deep breath and let myself get carried away with a sense of self-admiration. It felt like centuries had gone by since that infamous day, when, after badly swimming for a few meters, I found myself laid up in a stretcher.

The arrival of the latest group of amateurs distracted me from my thoughts. I began swimming again with a smile on my face, well aware of what I had achieved in my sports career.

One-half hour after leaving the shores of Pella, the density of the swimmers was now high again, just like at the beginning of the competition. That meant that the finish line was close. Just like meteors in space, other participants passed me proceeding in all directions, as if the finish line was spread out over various locations. To ensure that I was heading the right way and to avoid adding meters to an already very difficult crossing, I lifted my head to peek out of the water; then I dipped down again to finish my last few arm strokes. My eyes, which up until then had seen only yellow water, suddenly began seeing the bottom of the lake. Within a few moments, my nose was inches away from the bottom of the lake; then I realized that I had completed my adventure. I stood up and walked by the judges table, which annotated the number on my cap and announced my time, "Thirty-six minutes." To me, my time was just a minor detail because I was too much at the whim of my emotions to even activate the analytical part of my brain. I took a few more steps; then I stopped, took off my goggles and turned in direction of the lake to admire it in awe. I felt a chill running down my spine. My mind went around in circles; it kept repeating the same words, over and over: "Good job, Antonio. You made it!"

Concretely admiring the product of your work greatly increases your level of satisfaction. Visualizing the entire distance that I had swum made me feel very proud of myself. I had never felt like that before, not even after completing one hundred laps or 50 meters butterfly without breaks. And after just one week, I had the opportunity to do it all over again...

To make the next day's crossing more carefree and laid back, my friends and I decided to arrive on site the day before the event so we could go camping nearby. We all agreed that the month of July was the ideal time to sleep outdoors so, after enjoying some pizza, beer and old-fashioned dancing on the town square of Mandello del

Lario, surprising the middle-aged folks for whom the dancing was planned, we eventually made it to bed around 1 AM. Too bad that, after we laid down, we continued to laugh and play for the 'pleasure' of the other campers around us, who had no fun listening to our loud partying. When the night guard loudly threatened to kick us out, our campsite suddenly turned very quiet. Then slumber had the best of us. The best of everyone but me, that is, because, no matter how I turned, I couldn't sleep due to my uncomfortable air mattress, the confined space of being surrounded by four other people and the bothersome noise of widespread snoring; I really couldn't sleep. Around four o'clock, as I began feeling like I was on my way to a good night's rest, a terrible storm woke me up, once more making me as alert as if it were midday. As if that weren't enough, I began to feel cold. Hours went by; the storm moved away and the early sun rays kept me awake for a little while longer. My fears that I would be up all night become a certainty when my friends' alarms clocks began to ring. We slowly came out of our tents. Some had breakfast, while others headed to the bar to enjoy pastry and a cappuccino. As I know my body's digestion times very well, I opted for total fasting, telling myself, "The last thing I need is to get sick in the middle of the lake!"

When we arrived on the square, there was already a small line in front of the judges' tables. We set a meeting point and picked up our competition kits; then we were invited to board one of the many boats set up to transport the athletes to the opposite shore of the lake, where we were to begin our crossing. Just like Marines, we were dropped off on an embankment near the locality of Onno. We quickly took off our outerwear, placed it into the numbered sacks and we handed our sacks over to the boat operators. Once we were undressed, we realized that the outside temperature was brisk. That would have been inevitable because the previous storm could not but lower the outside temperature. Without hesitation, I opened the 'good' smelling large jar of lanolin and I generously spread grease all over myself, offering to share with all those who wished to smell like me. I looked around and noticed that the number of participants was decidedly higher than at the previous crossing; furthermore, everyone seemed to fear the low water temperature as everyone was wearing neoprene wetsuits. How strange... we looked around and felt like we were the only ones wearing nothing but a bathing suit!

A few minutes before the start, one guy from our group decided to get ready by doing an in-water warm-up. It was quite striking to see a big guy full of energy and muscles that normally dives in by doing a back-flip, hesitate as a girly man. "Guys, it's freezing!!!" said Daniele nicely. And I thought that if he felt cold... the rest of us were doomed. I gathered my courage and dipped my feet in the first few inches of water. For a moment, I felt like my feet were crumbling due to an unexplainable phenomenon. Avoiding attracting too much attention, I took a few steps back, re-opened the jar of lanolin and dipped my feet in it. Time flew by; the start signal would be sounded at any moment now. I felt the tension rising; I had the strange feeling that I had something to do, but I was running out of time. When the signal was sounded, it took me a bit by surprise. Around me I saw a mass of four hundred individuals run down the shore and jump into the lake waters. I stood there and enjoyed the scene, hesitating a bit longer. Once I realized that I was one of the few individuals still left on the shore, I gathered my courage and immersed myself in the lake, too. My impact with the water was a violent one. I felt like I had fallen into a refrigerator. I began swimming at a sustained pace, hoping that this would help raise my body temperature, but that 17°C water temperature seemed to be having the best of me. Within a few minutes, I realized that the situation was progressively worsening. The 400-meter deep pitch-black water was not what got me, although swimming in the darkness was certainly not my favorite thing to do; however, swimming in the cold water was getting progressively more painful and paralyzing. I began to feel pins and needles in my hands and feet and, to make matters worse, every time I placed my head under water my lungs froze up, making me hiccup. I quit trying to do the freestyle and, for a few meters, I did the breaststroke while keeping my head out of the water. I began to feel better. Then I submerged my head in the water and my lungs began to freeze up again. For a moment I threw a fit: Thus I reached the conclusion that it was time for me to transition to "panic!" mode, so I raised my hand to request the help of the rescue boat. The boat operators helped me get on board and then they offered me a blanket to warm up. With my head spinning and my teeth chattering, I continued shaking uncontrollably for several minutes. Then I thought, "What the heck just happened to me!?!"

Technically speaking, I suffered "thermal shock from cold water." Its symptoms include hypothermia, difficulty breathing, loss of conscience and cardiac arrest. If this series of symptoms comes on when you are in the water, drowning could be just around the corner. Subjects most prone to such conditions include thin people who, lacking a good layer of fat as thermal insulator under their skin, have a low resistance level in low temperature situations.

As I researched the scientific aspects of what had happened to me, I became aware of the various calculation mistakes I had made and how those mistakes could have cost me much more than a simple withdrawal from the competition. Despite all this, the most intense feeling that frazzled me was not linked to avoiding danger, but rather to the pain caused by not having reached my objective. For the moment, I decided to set that thought aside; however, I knew that sooner or later I would revisit it...

Four years had passed since the day I had given up on that swim and I still felt like I had left the job unfinished. Since my motivation revolved around making things fall where they belonged, I decided to try again, signing up once again for the Crossing of Lake Lario. To tell the truth, I had also tried last year, but the event was canceled due to the presence of logs in the lake due to inclement weather in previous days. However, it seemed that nothing would keep it from taking place as planned.

Just like four years earlier, I didn't attempt this crossing by myself; in fact, I went there with a group of friends, made up of eight swimmers, two supporters and one fiancée (mine). As usual, we decided to spend the evening before the swim not exactly like real athletes would do, e.g. stuffing ourselves with rich foods and drinking beer; but, most of all, participating in old-fashioned dances on the town square's dance floor and doing a really bad job at it. The experience was not exactly the same because I wanted to make some changes. For starts, as I hadn't forgotten about last time's sleepless night at the campground, this time I opted for a lovely Bed & Breakfast located in front of the lake. Second of all, instead of choosing the insanity of morning fasting, I woke up early and had a rich breakfast consisting of Melba toast and honey. Last but not least, instead of spreading myself with sheep grease from head to toe, I used a (much more effective) partial neoprene wetsuit. On the morning of the race, thanks to this preparation, I felt refreshed, rested and well equipped!

It was 8:30 AM when I arrived at the small port in Mandello del Lario. For a moment, I felt overwhelmed by the frenetic ways in which the organizers went back and forth to set up for the event. A bit reluctantly, I stood in line to pick up my competition kit and meal ticket; then, once again, I waited to catch a ride with one of the boats used as ferry service. I looked around and I felt like I was watching a familiar movie. I sat through the ferry ride, changed into my swim gear and placed my clothing in a numbered bag with a feeling of déjà vu. However, as I stood on the shore and waited for the competition to begin, I felt different: this time I was confident that I had done my best to prepare for the event. In this state of inner tranquility, I felt no need to concentrate on myself, so I could proceed to do something that I considered very useful: observe what others did. Those I observed first were those that spent time preparing their equipment, caring for it almost maniacally. I noticed that, judging from the expression on their faces, they were concentrated, serious and slightly tense. Very few of them were speaking. As I watched more closely, it seemed as if they were self-absorbed in performing a precise ritual, rather than simply preparing the equipment. I looked away and my attention was caught by a livelier group of swimmers, who were laughing and joking. At first sight, they looked like they were very relaxed; then, paying closer attention to how quickly they were talking and the slightly hysterical tone of their laughs, I gathered that their predominant mood was nervousness. They made me curious, so I tried to tune into their conversations. The most nervous guy in the group continued to ask questions like, "What happens if I get lost? What if I run out of breath? What can you see below the water?" It is obvious that his intentions were not to gather information, but rather to fill up on reassurance, involving his most willing friends to play parent in his psychological game. As I thought it over, the common thread among the various behaviors I had observed in the last few minutes was that they were all behaving more similarly to children than adults. And who knows? Maybe this was the secret behind masters swimming competitions: in a life made of important roles, tiring working days and unavoidable responsibilities, swimming gives us the opportunity to let out our inner child without running the risk of losing credibility in front of those who matter in our lives, allowing us to free our emotions just as they are, without a filter.

I looked down at my watch. The competition would begin soon. After the 10:30 ferry had come and gone, the judge officially announced the start of the crossing. Again, I thought back to four years earlier and felt an empty feeling inside, almost as if that memory needed to be tweaked. I realized that I was assuming a negative attitude, so I straightened my back, inhaled as much air as possible and, while holding my breath for a moment, I began feeling decidedly more relaxed and positive. I told myself that the only thing I knew for sure about today was that I would get to the other side with the strength of my arms and legs.

Minutes went by quickly. I spread the warming cream distributed by the event organizers all over my body; then, I closed my mini-wetsuit and entered the water up to my knees. I washed my face so I could begin to get used to the cold; then I looked for a favorable start position as I attempted to get ahead of most of the 600 participants. My heart began to throb, but my emotions remained steady.

Some of my friends positioned themselves in front of me. I let them. The starting judge began the countdown; then something strange happened. Two seconds before one could hear the start signal all participants had already jumped in the water, causing the most (theoretical) false start in history. The show must go on. Within a few seconds I found myself spinning my arms and legs as if I only had to swim a few hundred meters. I was submerged not only by the water that was fizzing around me, but also by dozens of feelings that I struggled to manage. The thought of my being cold tried to make its way into my mind, together with certain old fears, but this time I decided not to let them in, although they were incessantly knocking on the door of my mind while I fully devoted myself to elbowing those swimmers who were trying their best to pass me. I experienced some intense moments of very rough body contact. I had not foreseen this situation. Two swimmers boxed me in from the sides; another one tickled my feet, while the one in front of me, although decidedly slower than me, was in no way willing to allow me to pass him. At one point the situation became unbearable: the two swimmers at my sides begin to converge toward an undefined point ahead of me, and this resulted in me getting squashed in-between them. I tried to resist, intensifying my action, but a non-sportsman like hand rested on my left shoulder and violently pushed me back. Surprised, and a little scared, I slowed down for a moment and allowed this "nice" swimmer to slip by; then I regained my pace. About ten minutes after the start, the density of the swimmers decreased dramatically. By now, everyone was scattered throughout the lake, convinced that they had found the shortest way to reach the other shore. Although I found this surprising, I found myself shoulder to shoulder with my teammate Alberto, whom I had always thought of as unreachable in long-distance events. He was one of the few guys wearing a speedo and performing a distinctive stroke known as the "Alberto" arm stroke. We remained shoulder to shoulder for a few minutes. He was relentless, and I had no intention of quitting; in fact, as soon as I had the chance, I sped up and put some distance between us, knowing full well that, the day before, he had competed in another 6-kilometer crossing. He and he alone could do stuff like this! Twenty minutes after the start, my arms felt heavier and my breath shorter. The thought that I was approaching the finish line kept me going. I had a reverie, almost a vision: I envisioned myself coming out of the water and crossing the finish line; I was happy that I had made it; I was very proud of myself and smiled. At the end of this vision, my body shivered and, instead of feeling worn out, the shiver worked as a shot of adrenaline, reducing fatigue and allowing me to begin accelerating again.

After a few minutes, a smelled a strong odor of gasoline, which made me realize that I had entered the circle of boats positioned by the shore. Once I began seeing the bottom of the lake, I knew that I was finally done. I stopped; got up and walked in front of the judges' table, who recorded my time of 26 minutes by using an electronic system (I had a microchip attached to my ankle). I found myself surrounded by a crowd: approximately one hundred people, including spectators and athletes who had finished before me. I looked around to find my partner. Right when I saw her, she snapped a picture of me. Later, when I looked at that snapshot in the digital camera, I was amazed at how similar it looked to my mental picture of myself I had generated during the last few moments of my swim. Only then I felt like telling myself, "Great job, Antonio; you did it again!"

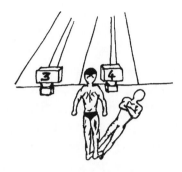

ANALYSIS - I am convinced

"Every living thing on this planet is growing and pursuing a goal. Once it reaches its goal and it is all grown up, it dies. If you are not growing, then you are dying; the opposite of life is death."
From Breathe the Dream by Alberto Lavenuta.

The conviction that one can always grow and improve is the essence of being human. When you quit believing that you can grow and improve, then you have given up and you are slowly dying. It is a principle that applies in every single setting in addition to life itself, helping you define one vision over another. If you convinced yourself that you can no longer improve, then you will never improve and you will begin to "die." If you convinced yourself that you can still improve, that you have much to do and that you still have much to experience and explore, then you will never run out of objectives and you will continue to mature. No age can prevent a human being from growing, and degrees of perfection may always be overcome. Great human beings are those who never stop growing as they believe that there is still one more path to follow...

On November 27, 1940, in the hour and year of the dragon, a boy was born at Jackson Street Hospital in San Francisco's Chinatown and he was initially named Li Yuen Kam; his name was later changed to Jun Fan, and the boy became known to everyone as Bruce Lee, man, an actor and athlete famous all around the world for having popularized Chinese martial arts among Westerners. Bruce Lee was profoundly convinced that, "Every day you have a unique possibility to surpass what you have done in the past and become better than you were yesterday." Until his death, which took place prematurely at the age of 32 in unclear circumstances, but officially classified as an allergic reaction to a pain killer, Bruce trained every day, considering his training time as rest time from life's activities. His daily routine consisted of various challenging series of abdominals, flexibility promoting exercises and running, which he integrated with bike riding, rope jumping and other exercises targeted to improve muscular concentration, speed and his skin's resistance to impact. He always said that, "If you get used to set limits in what you do, the sports you practice, your life and relationships, your actions will suffer from it, your surroundings will suffer from it and you will suffer from it as you will remain limited and confined to being a static rather than dynamic being. Limits do not exist; growth takes place at different levels and in phases. When you reach a higher phase, stay the course as long as possible and then move forward."

Swimming is a sport in which you primarily challenge yourself. In terms of this, you don't need an official competition to gauge how much you have grown because you can see it in every moment and during every practice. You just need to pay attention to your sensations if you wish to test your degree of gliding, the effectiveness of your stroke or your improved resistance to fatigue. If you want to base yourself on objective data, you just need to count the number of laps completed over a set period of time or the time it took you to complete a set number of repetitions. Of course, only participating in a competition you'll have the possibility to face your opponents, those who stand between you and a medal or just a team record, but if you are in the water and you are a masters level simmer, you are mainly challenging what is inside of you. The "masters' spirit" is just that: you set some goals, then you invest all the time and energy that you have, after work and family commitments, to exercise, practice and attempt to achieve your goals. When you succeed in overcoming your challenges, you feel a unique, indescribable sensation, which, on one hand, strengthens your self-esteem and, on the other hand, it pushes you to define higher and more ambitious goals. And if you avoid paying attention to the little voice in your head that continues to tell you to give up because what you are doing is dangerous, because there is no reason to do it, because in the end you won't really win anything, because all in all why should anyone do this (sometimes the little voice belongs to a familiar person), then you'll find yourself immersed in a sea of challenges though which you can achieve much joy. This joy is essential to find the energy you need to face issues, troubles and problems you will encounter during life on earth...

I had noticed him during warm-up because he swam in my lane. There was a master's level swimmer who was

different from the others; he had something more than the others. I immediately noticed him at the 50-meter freestyle event because, unlike the rest of the swimmers, he stood on the starting block focused and relaxed with the confidence of those who, no matter how things go, will always be fully content with himself. I saw him diving in with the rest of the swimmers in his heat and take off like a rocket, propelled by a powerful kick and the strength of only one arm. The other arm was missing its hand, so it could probably barely offer support. He performed super-quick flip-turns and he touched the wall setting a time of thirty-one seconds! Those who were there clapped warmly and they did it again later, when another guy, still in the 50-meter freestyle, competed as only few can do. He was not very tall; his legs and back were curved, keeping him from adopting a fully erect posture. I saw him climbing onto the starting block and take off with the others. At the end of the lane, his instructor waited for him to help him perform his flip-turn. Using a stick, the instructor touched the swimmer's head right when the swimmer was one-half meter away from the wall. Once the signal was received, the swimmer performed his flip-turn and he took off again, turning his hands and legs with joy and energy. At that exact moment I realized what was going on and I felt a shiver go down my spine, triggering emotions that went straight to my heart. My eyes watered up and it was hard to fight back tears when I understood that the boy, who evidently had physical challenges, was also blind. However, unlike most swimmers, he swam with vigor, enthusiasm, and so much energy. And when he touched the wall and finished his event, we all responded with a warm applause.

My mind kept dwelling on those images and emotions for the rest of the day. I thought of how fortunate I was to have had the opportunity to watch those two boys compete. I had too often focused on my limits, wrongly believing that they were insurmountable; now I understood that nothing could stop me if I pursued my goals with passion and love of life. Most of all, no negative outcomes could discourage me if I faced my challenges only thinking of enjoying the moment!

Swimming is a sport of feeling. Masters swimmers are people who, by spending a lot of time in their lanes, become used to being bombarded by elementary stimuli of a physical, emotional and mental nature. Outside the pool, masters' swimmers are people who experience increased appetite and an ever-growing desire to plunge into the water, which must necessarily be met by going to the swimming pool. Swimming is a unique experience: your body is completely immersed and hugged by a liquid; your skin feels touched, tickled and massaged all at the same time. Your aquatic experience is not only based on feeling cold and wet, but also on feeling light pressure and a unique state of gravity-free suspension. This special setting is reflected with extreme intensity within the internal world of the swimmer, who must interpret it, analyze it and face it constantly while performing his strokes, which, over time, become ever more tiring and technically imperfect. The swimmer's search for the ideal communion with water, which may coincide with an ever-increasing feeling of displacement speed, is every swimmer's greatest desire. In his heart, he dreams of one day being able to move with the elegance and speed of a dolphin.

If you swim, even only once a week, you will perfectly understand what I am talking about. If you don't know how to swim or if you haven't yet reached such a state of awareness, just know that it's just a matter of time and effort. I began almost from scratch and, at the beginning I listened with interest and skepticism to the ecstatic tales of those who swam. I too gradually uncovered that world of emotions of which I had heard from so many people. Day after day, I began to experience it, appreciate it and grant it an ever more important role in my life. I learned that as a fundamental component, fatigue is not a defect at all. In fact, that sense of muscular heaviness, together with shortness of breath and mental tiredness for having gone too many times back and forth, is the best part. When you exit the water and you know that you have given it your all, you experience an indescribable sense of wellness, although you may be feeling weak and unstable. When you are a master's level swimmer, you find it natural to seek this, even inside a competition. Because only competition can fully make you feel tremendously alive!

The 100-meter backstroke event did not go as planned. I was standing under a warm shower. I tried to relax and think of what could have gone wrong. In my head, I replayed the images from my competition, making an effort to focus on my errors. This required quite an effort because, as I warmed up in the heat of the shower and my muscles began to relax, I found it difficult to concentrate. I asked myself how I would find the mental strength to face my second challenge: I hadn't improved my time in the 100-meter individual medleys for over a year. While I am standing there, struggling with my thoughts, two swimmers in their fifties arrived next to me. Communal showers without stalls are not the best in terms of privacy, so, to remove myself from an embarrassing situation, I was driven to strike up a conversation with these perfect strangers. One of the two, with an easygoing tone, began to

say, "Nobody can keep me away from one of those amazing lunches!" I replied, "Lucky you; I am still running on an empty stomach! I can't wait to go eat, but first I have to do well in my second event." He replied, "Com'on, who cares? Will you get money if you improve your time?"

For a moment, I thought of his words, even because there was an element of truth in them. So it is: I am not getting paid for working hard. I am not getting paid for making an effort. I am not getting paid to get in the car, drive long distances, reach a pool far away from home and dive into a competition, which, regardless of how I do, will not bring any money. No, I am not getting paid at all. Does it matter? So I replied with a similar carefree tone, "Right, I am not getting paid for doing well on my event or set a personal record... but, on the other hand, you have no idea of how much this pays!" He smiled and nodded at me. I got him. He also put his heart and soul in these competitions, but he just said something at random, just for the heck of it, to play it cool. He too felt great pleasure in putting forth an effort in his competitions. I saw it in his eyes. I gathered it from his smile. Because he too is a masters level swimmer, just like me and all those who had come to compete in this unnamed meet in Liguria.

EMOTION
The opponent inside of me

It is odd to think that my most terrible opponent is inside a place that is very dear to me. When I seek him in my mind, he hides inside my heart. When I seek him in my heart, he hides inside my mind. He is a terribly skilled opponent; clever and almost unbeatable. He does not seek direct confrontation because that is not his way of facing me. He prefers attacking me when I am distracted, when I am not thinking of it or when I am busy doing something very important. Then he sneaks up behind me and begins yelling in my ears that I cannot make it, that I cannot give up and that, if I continue what I am doing, something bad would happen. Every time I cannot resist him, he wins, weakening my spirit. In fact, he feeds on my courage. He attacks me with fear, insecurity and defeat. He is the ruthless and capable opponent inside of me and he remembers all the bad things that have happened in my life. My opponent is cunning as he reminds me of my negative life experiences, making me think of them over and over, revisiting old feelings of inadequacy and endless uneasiness. My opponent is strong, very strong, but I became stronger than him because I understood that if I choose not to be brought down by my defeats, he cannot win over me; if I do not give up hope when the going gets tough, he cannot enjoy my misery; if I do not back out in front of a challenge, he has no power over me. To keep him quiet, I ignore him, laugh at him and tell him that I trust myself; so he'll lose, leave the room and disappear. Every time I win my challenges, whatever they may be, my opponent no longer lives inside me because he understands that there is no room left for him and his games. I am no longer scared of him!

EXERCISE

Below, write 3 challenges that you would like to conquer. In the second column, use a few words to write the reasons why you still haven't succeeded in conquering your challenge.

CHALLENGE   REASON

- ....
- ....
- ....

(e.g. challenge-learning to swim; reason-little time)

Now rate the challenges on a scale from 1 to 3, where 1 means more attainable, and 3 more demanding.

Once you are done, below write what you need to do, in terms of action and time, to win challenge number 1.

....
....
....
....

(e.g. looking for a swimming pool, going to sign up, organize activities...)

Now I will propose a challenge. Read these last few lines carefully. Start from the last item you listed and begin to make it happen. Next, advance to the next step. Then, move to the following step and so on. You will be surprised to discover how powerful it is to commit a challenge to a list of many items. In the end, taking a small step is mentally easier than envisioning having to face a big step, don't you think?

CHAPTER 8: FROM THE ITALIAN TO THE EUROPEAN CHAMPIONSHIPS

EXPERIENCE – Masters level endeavors

The following year, our team merged with another team so we now had two coaches, twice as many swimmers and our swim lanes inevitably ended up looking like frying pans stuffed with too many French fries. The most profound change regarded our lifestyle as master's level swimmers: in the past, our status was loosely defined but how our title was filled with competitive attributes. Rather than looking like swimmers, our new teammates glided through water like packs of sharks. Our practices became more intense, in terms of activity and variety. We began working on medleys, using pull-buoys, kickboards and hand paddles, as well as swimming an ever greater number of laps, which often reached one hundred forty (3.5 kilometers in one and one-half hours). The rhythm of training was frenzied: as soon as the swimmers in the fastest lane completed their training exercise, which on average required swimming 500 to 1200 meters, other swimmers were stopped regardless of what distance they had swum. Obviously, I was one of those swimmers who benefited from the shortened workouts, cutting it short, on average, by a couple of laps for each workout block.

I welcomed these changes with enthusiasm, even though some among us perceived them as unbearable and inappropriate. The first thing I decided to tune into was the new mentality, so, when I was in the water, I too began acting like I were a shark. I was convinced that I was fortunate for having followed an unusual path in my swimming experiences as this made it easier for me to find a good reference point to follow and surpass. In other words, many fellow swimmers represented many roles models to emulate and winning strategies to copy.

Swimming practice turned into an authentic collective fight for survival, in which the only rule that mattered was to give it our all, while attempting to stay alive through the one-and-one-half-hour training sessions. I realized that I was constantly in touch with my limits because every time I had to undergo suffering, face moments of crisis, clench my teeth and fight back against a sense of dreadful fatigue. All this seriously challenged my body and mind, especially when the latter was drilled by the typical loser's phrase, "What are you doing all this for?"

Now that I was convinced to have grown a fin on my back, I decided to act like the others and be cut-throat to overcome all sorts of obstacles. The approach I adopted is commonly known as the "master's spirit," a way to experience your time in the pool with a constant drive to improve and surprise yourself. During this phase of my life as a swimmer, I did something that was fundamental to preserve my will to challenge myself, something that some do sub-consciously, but that too many don't do at all and they end up giving up before they can even become real masters swimmers. This psychological approach consists in serenely accepting your current ability level, while positively believing that you can improve it with strong will, commitment and sacrifice. I decided to accept the fact that I was "temporarily inadequate" because in my heart I was certain that with passion, endurance and by maintaining an open mind I would continue to improve and see my efforts rewarded by many tiny moments of happiness. So I began signing up for events that went way beyond the usual 50- and 100-meter freestyle…

After only two months from the beginning of my new "era," I attempted competing in the 1500 meter freestyle event. When my new teammates suggested the idea, I told myself, "Why not? I have already swum that distance when I crossed Lake Orta, so it can't be much worse than I have already experienced in open waters." My friend Totò must also have performed a similar exercise in self-persuasion as, like me, he also swam that event for the first time. The event organizers explained to me that, to avoid making the meet run long and into the evening hours (over two hundred swimmers signed up for the 1500 meter freestyle), each lane would host two swimmers, instead of one. Totò and I would share the same lane; one wearing a red cap and the other wearing a black cap and, oddly enough, each respectively swimming up and down the left and right sides of the lane. This is the only way masters swimmers can compete in long-distance events since the first heats may last over an hour (when feeling worn out, older masters swimmers –aged 60 to 70 years old– switch to double-arm backstroke and breaststroke as this is allowed in a "freestyle" event). The pool's lanes were quite large so there should be no issues with frontal collisions.

Finally the event took place. As usual, the first problem I had to face is to keep count of thirty Olympic-size laps because, during one-half hour of swimming without lap counters, my brain could crash and lose all my lap-count data! This is no minor issue; in fact keeping a good lap count during a competitive event matters to many masters swimmers. However, I was reassured by the thought that, two laps before the end of my event, the judge would let me know by blowing the whistle in my face during my flip-turn.

To avoid running out of energy right when I needed it the most, at the beginning of the meet, I decided to swim my initial laps at a moderate speed. My strategy revealed itself flawed as all the other red caps disappeared ahead of me. I told myself that I didn't care and that, since I started with this strategy, I must stick to it: "Stroke, stroke and breathe... stroke, stroke and breathe."

Half way through the meet, I switched gears and increased my speed, also because I felt like I had been in the water for hours. When I had exactly four laps left to the finish, I tried my best at what I like to think is sprinting as I felt like I had enough energy saved up. In the last two laps, punctually signaled by the line judge, I gave it my all, spinning my arms and legs to the best of my ability. And, right at second to the last lap, Totò and I performed the best show of the meet: a frontal collision with a most memorable head-butt. We stopped, looked in each other's faces a bit surprised; then we dipped our heads back under water and we continued to swim to complete our event, both of us completing it in a little less than 30 minutes. After exiting the pool, Totò and I couldn't seem to stop laughing.

My master's swimmer spirit was constantly growing. Over the next few months, I took on the 200-meter freestyle, 200 breaststroke and 100 individual medley, events during which I experienced strong emotions and a lot of fun. I complimented myself; I told myself, "good job" just for having tried. I was always proud of what I was able to achieve, although the standings always relegated me to the bottom of the list. Oh well, since I hadn't considered this aspect as relevant to my satisfaction. On the other hand, I found it fundamental to update my results sheet, whose looks had by now dramatically improved since I had recreated it using my computer. It was now a huge Excel spreadsheet, which contained all my event times from all my meets, showcasing all my personal records in red and my specific distance (25 and 50 meters) in bolded numbers. One day, as I was closely looking over the spreadsheet, I felt like putting it side by side with my Advent calendar. The spreadsheet image reminded me that, when I was in elementary school, we always had an advent calendar in our classroom. Every day, our teacher selected a most deserving student, and the selected student was allowed to open the tiny daily calendar window and eat the chocolate it contained. Incidentally, I never got to eat the chocolate from the advent calendar. As I was taken over by the desire to fill as many boxes as possible, and also to fulfill that desire for chocolate, which I had never been able to earn before, I signed up for the 50 meter butterfly. Big mistake! The butterfly, also known as the dolphin-kick stroke, is a very difficult stroke to master if you never really acquired the proper technique. I told myself that, in the end, 50 meters couldn't be all that bad!

I was on the starting block of my first 50-meter butterfly

competition and I was very nervous. The entire team was lined up at the edge of the pool and everyone was looking at me. Among my new teammates, there were some who, not knowing me very well, and, confiding in my tiny muscles, thought that I had the ability to amaze. To a certain extent, you couldn't blame them. The start of the competition came suddenly and painfully, as if I were getting whipped on the back. I dove in and planed over the water with my stomach, keeping my legs spread open and my knees virtually bent. Those looking at me from the outside thought that I may have hurt myself, but I was used to dive in like this, like a rolling stone. I made the best of my underwater work to carry out the strategy I had planned a few days earlier, consisting of staying under water as much as possible and advance as many meters as I could without swimming. When I emerged, I sadly realized that I had only advanced a few meters rather than the eight-ten meters I was hoping for. I began squirming around as I thought butterfly should be swum, shaking my arms and splashing water everywhere. When I reached the end of the lap, I had a feeling that the return lap would have something in store for me. I touched the edge of the wall, turned 180°, took a breath and plunged back into the water for a new attempt at apnea. Go, go and go! Those seconds felt like years and those meters felt like kilometers. For a moment, I had the impression that my entire life played in front of me. While swimming in this sort of competition trance, I ended up forgetting the first fundamental rule of swimming: breathe only when your head is out of the water. And so I drank an abundant mouthful of water. I didn't give up; in the end, I am an expert: I swallowed and coughed a little, but then I fought back and intensified my action. When I was about ten meters away from the end of the competition, and regardless of the enormousness of the effort, for a few seconds I felt like I was not advancing. I felt like Rocky Balboa knocked out after a series of punches by Ivan Drago. My vision turned foggy and my arms felt heavy: I was having trouble pushing my hands forward during the recovery phase to begin a new rotation. At any rate, I successfully reached my destination. I touched the touchpad and the chronometer showed 47 seconds. My heart was racing, and I thought, "I am still alive!" One of my teammates "kindly" yelled, "Antonio, you suck!!!"

In addition to maintaining your body in good physical shape, training regularly is the key to improve your muscle memory of stroke technique. Surely, your muscles must be set up correctly because otherwise you end up memorizing a movement full of defects, not very effective and, over the long run, even difficult to correct. For this reason, my coach kept repeating, "You have to watch your technique." I repeated it in my head, saying, "I must improve my technique, especially in butterfly and backstroke." However, asserting yourself doesn't necessarily mean succeeding in doing it; despite my effort, this is why I kept repeating the same mistakes. My main mistake was my own personal approach: I should have stopped telling myself, "Relax, keep swimming and you'll end up learning," because that approach does not work. On the other hand, I should have asked myself the right questions, like, "How can I improve my technique? Which exercises should I perform?" Unfortunately, my timing in realizing these things was not quite right, so for the time being I decided to set aside any butterfly competitions.

Half way through the season I began hearing talk of a winter camp. Here's how it was pitched: "You pack your suitcase, come to Riccione, attend two-hour practices over five days and then you'll go home a happy man." "Alright," I said, purposely focusing on all the entertainment and social opportunities of the entire deal.

My expectations were met. Together with many nice people, some of whom brought spouses and children, I spent pleasant moments made of long conversations, lively lunches, walks along the beach and, of course, practices involving swimming for approximately 5 kilometers. After swimming like never before in my life, suffering cramps, shoulder pain and inflammations that I thought I had finally overcome, I returned to Milan feeling like canned tuna rather than swimming faster than a dolphin. The only part of my body that seemed to have experienced any improvement was my heart, strengthened by all the positive emotional experiences. At my now old age of 32, it didn't often happen to me to experience a whole week of living like a real athlete, which involved waking up at seven o'clock, eating a light breakfast, followed by morning practice.

After returning from such an experience and with a master swimmer's spirit that had by now reached incredible peaks, I was convinced that I could now swim the 800-meter freestyle event. No worries, it was obviously achievable, especially after having competed in longer distances; the issue was that this events seemed to be a halfway event for which I was not sure whether I should swim fast and run the risk of exhausting all my energy or pace myself and hope not to arrive too refreshed at the finish line.

A few days before the competition, an unfortunate injury made it an easy decision. Half way through a lap of butterfly, one of my back muscles contracted violently, making me feel excruciating pain. I experienced a deep, burning sensation; in my imagination, I felt like I had been locked by two large hooks under my shoulder blades. I stayed in the water, facing down, paralyzed by the pain of this new contraction. I exited the pool moving like Robocop: some laughed at me while others looked worried. My coach sent me to take a hot shower. This was the pits, as I already knew that it would take time and patience to recover from this. It would certainly be days before I could go back in the water, but I wouldn't quit. I went to see Roberto, a tall and big osteopath, who gave me back treatments over a couple of sessions of excruciating pain and told me to perform a couple of exercises. It was simply a miracle; within a week I was back in the water and I was able to swim in the 800-freestyle event. My fear of my back pain returning certainly made me face the competition with care, but, in the end, I felt happy because, if on one hand I was able to check off an empty box in my spreadsheet, on the other hand I set a time that was easy to beat.

Toward the end of the season, as icing on the cake, the team announced that we would be participating in the Italian Masters Swimming Championships. When I first heard the news I felt a bit of hesitation; then I told myself something that encouraged me, "In the end, it can't be much different from any other meet! There will certainly be a few more participants, a little longer to wait, but considering that even on this occasion I didn't run the risk of missing out on a medal, what was there to be worried about?" I willingly accepted the idea, making it my goal to set my personal records in the 50-meter freestyle, 200-meter freestyle and 100 meter breaststroke. As the meet drew closer, we decided to prepare with a second camp, during which I successfully achieved optimal physical conditions. By the beginning of July, I was pumped up, toned and ready to face my competitions as fierce as ever; then, when I set foot in

Riccione, where the Championships were being held, the easygoing atmosphere of summer made me feel totally relaxed so much so that my mind and body were mutually convinced to be on vacation. I shook myself up to gather energy and concentration, but it was only before my event, when I saw my name on the scoreboard, that the right state of mind came back to me.

Despite the short-lived crisis and the great effort made to snap out of it, I succeeded in reaching all three goals. With great satisfaction in my heart, and after a long year of practice, injuries, challenges and victories, I granted myself a well-deserved rest period over the summer.

The beginning of the new season was marked by a new change. As I realized that I could never improve continuing down the path of merely making an effort, I put myself in condition to systematically overcome all my personal limits. And that's exactly what happened. Ever convinced that I could improve my past performances, every time I participated in a new competition, I took home a new personal record. The secret behind my newly improved attitude was Claudia, who had been my lifetime partner for a few months now. With Claudia by my side, I felt grown-up, balanced and secure. Claudia wanted to be there for all my meets because she wanted to support me and welcome me with a smile and a hug after each event, whether I did well or not. All this gave me strength and tranquility, creating a sense of completeness that I had never felt before. I felt more mature and ready to face anything. For this reason, at the end of the season, when they opened up registration for the European Masters Swimming Championships in Slovenia, I had no hesitation to accept the challenge. Too bad that, due to some organizational changes made by the team's officials, our master swimmers spirit was no longer the same. Many team members, who for a long time had transmitted enthusiasm and inspired me to challenge myself, lost their drive and decided to not participate. Only I and three other fearless athletes participated in the international competition...

The facility that hosted the event was large, but the parking lot was barely large enough to hold half the vehicles arriving for the event. With a little luck, I found a small spot in between other vehicles and, after grabbing my swim bag, I headed toward the entrance. Tall barriers hid what was happening inside the pool area. Only the high and colorful flags fluttering above suggested that an international event was being held inside. The stadium was buzzing, vaguely reminding me of the sound of a soccer match. Then, at one point, I heard a roar. My legs froze with emotion and they began to tremble. Then I heard the whistle of the head judge, followed by the unmistakable metallic voice pronouncing the phrase, "Take your marks..." beep! I couldn't see anything from where I was standing, but my heart seemed to have understood everything so much so that it began pounding inside my chest.

I felt curious and afraid to visually discover what was happening inside. As if attacking me from behind, a voice inside me said something strange and unexpected, "You, why did you come here to the European Championships of Masters Swimming?"

I lost all my confidence. The event was impressive and very important. I had the feeling that I had bitten off more than I could chew and I had jumped into a competition that was way above my abilities. All this led me to believe that it would not be easy for my name and times to show up in the rankings. So stated, this may sound ridiculous, but, unlike national meets, where all athletes participating in an event are systematically entered in the rankings, international event scoreboards only include the names of those few "privileged" ones whose time is below qualifying time; all the others can do is accept the disgrace of having the anonymous and mortifying acronym NT printed next to their name. NT stands for No Time, which, in other words means, "Hey, loser, why in the heck did you come?!?"

Purposely to avoid such embarrassment, I opted to sign up for only two events, rather than the five individual events allowed for each participant. I aimed for competing in the 50- and 100-meter freestyle competitions, in which I was confident that I could make the rankings, although up until then I had never been able to swim as fast as required to meet qualification times. So naturally, this obvious question should follow: what makes you think that you can make it this time? The answer: part recklessness and part confidence in my will to succeed, also in light of the excellent work carried out last August, praised by my coach during my latest tests.

Among the four participants from my team, I appeared to be the most in shape and most focused; however, instead of taking advantage of this situation, I was taken over by an unbearable stress level, which I couldn't seem to manage. As if that weren't enough, the long car ride to the meet physically wore me out, so, at the time I entered the water, I felt nervous and insecure…

At that moment, I felt like I was in a movie, in one of those scenes where everything moves in slow motion. I was in the pool, stopped at the end of my lane; I felt breathless and my heart was pounding. I had just ended my second

and last event at the European championships. Before exiting the water, I still had to perform an important task: to check if, at least in the 50-meter freestyle, I had achieved my goal of making it into the rankings. The previous day's event had not gone well. For the 100-meter freestyle, I had swum with all my strength; however, I had barely improved my personal best and this wasn't enough to avoid being labeled as No Time. I stretched out my neck to see the electronic scoreboard. I took off my goggles so I could see better, but all I could see by squeezing my eyes were luminous numbers. I read thirty-one seconds and something. I relaxed my facial muscles and, feeling disappointed, I immersed myself under water, with the imaginative hope that I could drown my loss. Not only had I set a time one second higher than the required qualification time, but I had also not improved my personal best. I felt completely defeated.

I grabbed the step ladder and climbed out of the pool to go pick up my clothes, feeling so low that, if I had dog ears, I would have looked like a Cocker Spaniel. It came natural to ask myself if this was indeed the absolute best I could do. One of my teammates approached me and distracted me from my thoughts, defining my performance unbalanced and meaningless. I kept quiet. I couldn't say anything. I didn't feel like moving on from this defeated state of mind, also because the fact that feeling sorry for myself almost felt good. Then, although I didn't know why, I felt like looking up to the sky. For a moment, the sun blinded me and my body began to shake. I felt an intense sense of warmth and peace. When I reopened my eyes, it felt natural to tell myself, "I will again never feel so low after having failed! Every time you do not win, think back to how you were at the beginning." One second later, I identified my biggest mistake: having forgotten my past.

Exactly seven years ago, I was dragged out of the pool by a coach because I felt light-headed and close to passing out. Back then, if somebody had told me, "Come on, relax, in 7 years you will be participating in the European Championships," I probably would have suggested for him to go see a psychiatrist. On the other hand, here I was, swimming with athletes that had been swimmers for most of their lives or that dedicated their lives to swimming. I was like them; I was one of them. This made me proud and it really was what mattered for me that day.

I was very disappointed that I had failed to reach my goals. Sometimes I even casually considered the idea of retiring from competitive swimming and just swimming to stay fit. I had never experienced failure in such a direct way, therefore the pain I felt was unfamiliar and intense. However, I did not quit. So what allowed me to erase all traces of defeat and to overcome such a tough moment?

I have bad news for you: erasing a memory from your mind is something that can't be done. You can certainly choose not to think about it; you can tell yourself that it has never happened; you can suppress it into your subconscious and, in extreme cases, you can even start to drink or smoke to forget, but don't worry: sooner or later, that memory will come back to you because it is now inside of you and it belongs to you. This happens for a simple reason: defeats, together with victories, make up your experience. Your experiences enable you to know what works and what doesn't. At the right time, your experiences will resurface so you can avoid repeating the same mistakes. This is nothing new, also because the following question still stands: if you can't erase a defeat, how can you quickly overcome it? You can do so by simply focusing your attention on something else, on a different image, which you connect with a positive state of mind. When I saw 31 seconds displayed on the scoreboard, for a moment I felt like that number had burned into my retina. I saw 31 everywhere I went. And the more I saw it, the sicker I got. Then, almost as if the sun had wanted to awaken me from that state, I suddenly saw an image of myself lying on a bed in the infirmary of the swimming pool on the first day of swim lessons. My heart ached; then it felt natural to say, "Heck, until a few years ago, I couldn't even complete a lap of freestyle; now look how far I have come!" This allowed me to take on a positive state of mind and it made me redefine my defeat as something unimportant. At that point, I no longer felt down, but quite the opposite.

This technique may be used at any time in your life, for any occasion. When you are on the beach and you are complaining about the heat, try to focus your attention on something else: for example, think of how much harder it would feel to endure that temperature in the city. A moment later, you will realize how fortunate you are to be there, laying out at a stone's throw from the beach, while your friends are back in the city, working in unbearable temperatures. This is just an example, but I am certain that you now understand the technique of how to switch images in your head to release a negative emotion and achieve a positive one. In the end, the choice rests with you.

When things do not go as you want, you may feel like you are drowning in quicksand. You can decide whether to complain about your bad luck and letting yourself go, giving up all you have, or react, fight, try to identify a handhold to grab on to, begin to pull yourself out of the mud and return to living and growing. Every trial holds a positive and a negative side. If you learn to look at the positive side, you will begin to live a better life.

ANALYSIS – The world of masters swimming

Italian masters swimmers are among the best in the world. Membership amounts to approximately 12,000 with countless meets held around the country, both in and out of the pool. The average age of master swimmers ranges from 30 to 45, although the M50 and M55 age groups have quite a few participants, as well. On average, master swimmers train three times a week, supervised by one or more coaches. They love their competitions and they are so faithful to their duties that, if they have to miss practice because their job keeps them away, they take cap and goggles with them and go swimming anywhere they can.

Many masters swimmers took on swimming as adults and, after having learned to swim a good number of laps and developing a passion for swimming, they began participating in competitive swimming and experiencing how nice it feels to improve one's performance. These master swimmers are most admirable and tenacious.

Other masters swimmers learned to swim as children; they participated in competitive swimming when they were young adults but then, for one reason or another, they quit swimming. Years later, they found their way back to swimming either because they could no longer stay away from it or because they realized that the rolls around their waistlines began to appear too visible. These master swimmers are the most skillful and successful…

I had noticed him at previous meets. It was inevitable because, after his performances, the announcer usually announced, "…he set the new national record for his age group." Meet after meet, I learned to recognize him in the water, among the athletes selected for the last heat. I still remember that, in a previous competition, I had nicknamed him the "Golden Man" because he wore gold-colored jammers, whose design was later banned by international regulations. This time, we had the opportunity to have a short conversation and he seemed like a forty-year-old master swimmer, as I have seen others, driven to swim and determined to swim well.

Then we had a closer meeting at the Italian Championships in the 200 individual medley event; he was in the last heat of the M40 age group, while I was in the first heat of the M35. On that occasion, I had observed him memorize his exercises during dryland training. The most striking thing about him was the way he held the straps of his goggles between his teeth, almost if he was getting ready to bite the water and not only swim in it. When he dove in, I was sitting on a chair behind his starting block, waiting for my turn to swim. As usual, upon his arrival at the swimming arena, the organizers had announced his latest world record for the M40 age group. Then, one day, I decided I wanted to learn more about Alberto Montini's past...

In the eighties and nineties, Alberto was a young star in Italy's swimming scene. He had swum alongside talented athletes such as Sacchi, Lamberti, Gleria and Michelotti. In his long career, he had also been trained by the amazing Mr. Castagnetti, coach to the national team and Italian swimming sensation Federica Pellegrini. Coach Castagnetti had now been deceased for some time.

After he retired from the sport, Alberto did not swim for a long time, losing his shape and even becoming a smoker. Then, one day, he looked at himself in the mirror and, noticing that he did not look like he wanted, he spontaneously said to himself, "I don't like what I have become. That's it." He quit smoking; returned to swimming and began competing in master level competitions, scoring many consecutive victories, as well as countless national and world records for his age group. What's his secret? As he himself would tell you, all is made possible by a normal lifestyle, which includes family, hobbies and sport. This is why he mostly practices during his lunch break, so that he can be home in the evenings to have dinner with his family members.

In the pool, Alberto trains as a dedicated, committed and resolute swimmer, motivated by a deep love of swimming and drive to meet his objectives. This is Antonio's spirit; it is the spirit of all of today's master swimmers who, just like me, live with the same intensity as Alberto the good experience of master's level competitions, although they do not have the skills needed to reach competitive levels.

Those who begin competitive swimming as adults have a less polished technique, less ease in swimming and, on average, worse times than master level swimmers with past competitive experiences. Besides this, one cannot really tell the difference between a "master swimmer" and the next swimmer because, for the most part, we all have common characteristics.

First of all, master swimmers have a big passion for swimming. By definition, they are adults who go to the pool driven by their personal desire to practice a sport and stay in shape. Sometimes they go back to swimming following their doctor's advice; while other times it may be a friend or their conscience that tells them that their physical condition could only improve with physical activity. On the other hand, some master swimmers have been swimming all their lives and they have never quit. A second characteristic that distinguishes master level swimmers is their will to put forth commitment, almost as if they were training for the Olympics. After a day's work and while managing a million family and personal issues, the master swimmer enters the pool to practice for one to two hours, during which he swims kilometers and takes on technical, resistance and speed testing. The master swimmer's heartbeat ranges between 130 and 180 beats per minute, according to activity level and age. When you are performing training repetitions at the age of 12 or 18, recovery times are quick; young athletes need only a few seconds to repeat the same exercise almost with the same amount of energy. At the age of 35 or 50, recovery times are very long, so much so that, when you need to take off again after a break, you are never sure if you will succeed in completing your exercise.

Then the swim meets come. Most masters level swimmers love competition because they know that their true challenge is not against an opponent or for a medal. Although these aspects may increase the swimmers' motivation, master swimmers race against themselves and their past performances. One must also bear in mind that time is a factor that works against master swimmers because the older you are, the harder it is to improve. However, every five years, moving up to the next age group and starting all over with a different set of qualification times is a nice way to gain a new level of motivation. The wide choice of events (50-, 100-, 200-, 400-, 800 and 1500-freestyle; 50-, 100- and 200 butterfly, breaststroke and backstroke and 100-, 200-, and 400- individual medleys) contributes in getting motivated as well, and, in fact, it enables everyone to find a new objective, even if achieving it may take years.

Another variable that adds an element of challenge for all ages is the points system. When a master swimmer participates in a meet, his/her performance is recorded in the National database, including event times and points earned. Points are calculated by mathematical comparison between your finals time and your qualification time (normally close to the world record for your master age group). This means that if a 70-year-old man (class M70) takes 34 seconds to swim 50-meter freestyle with a qualifying time of 27.70 seconds, he will earn approximately 800 points. If a 31-year old man (class M30) swims the same distance in the same time, he would earn only 660 points because his qualification time is approximately 22 seconds. This has an important implication: master swimmers compete with all others, although they may belong to different categories. In fact, with the exception of Italian or international championships, all meet events are set up by time rather than age group...

Claudio was few meters away from me. He wore his competition suit, robe, knee-high socks and a pair of fun yellow rubber clogs. We ended up in the same heat of our

100-meter breaststroke event in the Regional Champs of Lombardy; we were both in the middle lanes, right next to each other. I was a bit nervous. We had chatted several times because he was always nice and helpful. Three years earlier, in Varedo, I had admired him as he set the world record for the 200 breaststroke for his age group. I still remember that, that day, the 200 breaststroke were not in the meet announcement; however, at one point the officials had taken a break to allow Claudio and two other rather young and vigorous guys to enter the water. The announcer had introduced the event as an "attempt to set a new world record," and the two young men would swim alongside Claudio to set pace for him. When, at the end of his event, the stopwatch stopped 7 seconds before the previous world record, everyone attending, excitedly and enthusiastically began to clap and shout his name. That day, Claudio had seemed like a giant!

Shortly, we would compete against each other. He smiled, undressed and grabbed his swim cap and goggles. We climbed on the starting blocks and dove in. For the duration of the event, it felt like Claudio was my shadow. I gave it all my muscle power and energy, but he resembled a torpedo as he swam quietly and compactly. At the end of the race, I touched the wall barely before he did. I was so worn out that I could feel my heart pulsating in the back of my throat; on the other hand, he barely seemed tired. I observed him while he curiously looked at the stopwatch; then he exited the pool and flaunted his usual composure. I had certainly heard him grumble before for a time that was below his expectations, but Claudio Negri is always extraordinary. It's not by chance that he is a friend to some, a father to others and, to a few, even a grandfather; to everyone, Claudio is a class 1936 masters level swimmer, who holds several national and world records.

Every week from October to May, the calendar of masters swimming events includes several events, both in the North and South of the country. On average, participants range from 600 to 1000 swimmers and can sometimes reach 1500 swimmers at the Desenzano and Riccione meets. At every meet, the atmosphere is always the same: anxiety, focus on the faster heats, happiness for a personal record and excitement for an exceptional performance; plus, you experience fun, friendship and sharing of similar experiences. After an event, it's generally customary for a master swimmer to talk about his time, his feelings and things he could still improve before he can reach his preset objective. It is also customary to hear him wrap up his conversation with the usual phrase, "Alright, guys, it's finally the time we were all anxiously awaiting: let's all go get a good meal!"

The masters swimmers you meet all have the same beaming look that reveals how much they love swimming. You can easily tell them apart from those few swimmers who look excessively worried, stressed and disgusted for what they have to do as if they had been forced to compete because of a threat. They are those swimmers who still haven't caught the essence of the master swimmer's spirit. Once they too will understand that a swim meet is a time of testing and personal growth, they will begin to change, mature and improve. When they too will understand that a masters swimming meet is the time during which a swimmer reaps what he or she sows during practice, then they will also begin to work harder during the entire time they spend in the pool, together with their most tenacious teammates. When they too will understand what it means to feel the master swimmer's spirit, then their attitude before a meet, practice and any trial in life will also change. They too will always smile, feel relaxed and remain ready to enjoy all those moments that bring opportunities to feel alive.

EMOTION
Ask them what it is

If you want to know what the spirit of the master swimmer is, ask one of us. You will see the swimmer's eyes light up and she will smile at you. After a moment of hesitation, she will tell you:

"See, dear friend, the spirit of the master swimmer is what makes you fully experience the sport you practice. For me, it's swimming. If I don't go to the pool at least three times a week, I begin feeling like I am missing something important, something that gives me balance. To me, swimming is a physical need, a need to touch water, but also a need to make contact with my inner self. I need to swim to get tired and I give it my all in practice. I need to spend time with my teammates, breathing chlorine-filled pool air. I need to share my passion for swimming with other swimmers. I need to compete to verify that the effort I put into my training yields results. I need to compete because competition makes me feel indescribable emotions. These are the reasons why I get up early on Sunday morning. When I open my eyes, I immediately think of the wave of satisfaction that will run through my body at the end of the meet. When I look at my time on the scoreboard, I feel my inner self relax. At that moment, after many sacrifices and commitment, I have a feeling of well-being and complete fulfillment. I am at peace with myself, with others and the rest of the world. When I touch the wall at the end of my race, it's a bit like if my heart was smiling. There, this is the spirit of master swimmers. But take my advice: do not take my word for it. To truly understand what this spirit is, try it as a first-hand experience."

EXERCISE

Use these examples to create your own personal table

MASTERS – TABLE OF PERSONAL RECORDS

Category	Date	Meet	Points	25m Lap Personal Best	Speciality	50m Lap Personal Best	Points	Meet	Date	Category
					50Free					
					100Free					
					200Free					
					400Free					
					800Free					
					1500Free					
					50Back					
					100Back					
					200Back					
					50Breast					
					100Breast					
					200Breast					
					50Fly					
					100Fly					
					200Fly					
					100IM					
					200IM					
					400IM					

MASTERS – TABLE OF RESULTS

50Free		100Free		200Free		400Free		800Free		1500Free	
season 1		season 1		season 1		season 1		season 1		season 1	
25mt	50mt	25mt	50mt	25mt	50mt	25mt	50mt	25mt	50mt	25mt	50mt
season 1		season 1		season 1		season 1		season 1		season 1	

50Fly		100Fly		200Fly		100IM		200IM		400IM	
season 1		season 1		season 1		season 1		season 1		season 1	
25mt	50mt	25mt	50mt	25mt	50mt	25mt	50mt	25mt	50mt	25mt	50mt
season 1		season 1		season 1		season 1		season 1		season 1	

50Breast		100Breast		200Breast		50Back		100Back		200Back	
season 1		season 1		season 1		season 1		season 1		season 1	
25mt	50mt	25mt	50mt	25mt	50mt	25mt	50mt	25mt	50mt	25mt	50mt
season 1		season 1		season 1		season 1		season 1		season 1	

AMATEUR - TABLE OF GOALS AND PERSONAL RECORDS

Test type	Outcome	Date
Example: *swim 40 laps non-stop*	*Example:* *Time recorded*	

CHAPTER 9: THE IRON MASTER

EXPERIENCE – A journey that lasts 18 events

I was not born to swim; however I fell in love with this sport. I was not born to compete in swim meets; in fact, until the age of 30, the thought of doing anything like that hadn't even crossed my mind. However, every time I competed, I experienced very strong emotions. Seven years after my first swim lesson, although my technique needed to improve, my endurance needed to be fine-tuned and my swim times could only drop, I felt like a winner: I succeeded in beating that little vicious voice that kept pushing me to quit everything. I succeeded in becoming a Master swimmer and join a team. I succeeded in turning a health need into authentic passion. The end result was that now I felt good, I couldn't stay away from the water and I found out that, besides new moms and elderly ladies, there were other pleasant people to meet at the pool. I met my life partner, Claudia, at the pool. At the time, she was merely a "summer participant" in my practice lane. Now, she loves the sport so much that she wants to be there for all my meets. Needless to say, I had to travel a long journey before receiving so much support and love! In a certain way, I had to face a challenge as tough at the Olympic Games. But, at the end of my marathon, which lasted exactly seven months of courtship, I won the most precious medal of all: her heart…

On the day I first saw her at the edge of the lane, I almost felt like I was experiencing a mirage: her long, light hair fluttered slowly at the sound of music; her gorgeously contagious smile glowed in every direction; her elegant and mellow behavior was to my eyes like the rippling waves of the sea. "It's her; I'll introduce her to you," said my friend, who had been adamantly trying to hook us up; my friend was convinced that Claudia and I were made for one another. Then, nature took its course. I made a joke, Claudia smiled and we spent an evening with friends. I thought that after three months of knowing each other, it was time to go on our first date, so I sent her a text message with a joke, combined with an invite to meet up somewhere. She nicely replied, "That's funny; but as far as going out for drinks, I don't think so." I did not give up.

For a few months we continued getting together with friends or meeting up for short meetings, such as during our coffee breaks. I took on the most difficult challenges in order to see her: skating or driving on fresh snow: all to no avail. She kept slipping away from my hands, like a very slippery fish. Then, at New Year's Eve, things seemed to be improving.

We ended up spending that night together, although we were surrounded by ten other people. On that occasion, I revealed my feelings for her, delivering the most difficult speech of my life, in the most complicated conditions ever, caused by one too many drinks. She seemed happy to hear my words, although I spoke to her while lying down on a bed, white as paper and with a wet towel on my head. I thought that I was very close to her heart; but then, nothing happened.

We stayed away from each other for a few weeks and took a pause of reflection; then, on a day in February, we spent the day together on Lake Como, and finally it was just the two of us! We had lunch in Brunate, took a stroll along the lake and enjoyed hot chocolate on a boat. Incredibly, she kept resisting me, keeping me at arm's length, as if we were magnets of the same polarity. However, when I drove her home that night, after seven months of holding my breath, I received that bit of fresh air I had been waiting for: our first kiss.

Strengthened by the support of my wonderful Claudia, who never quit encouraging me and cheering me on from the stands, for the new swim season, I decided to set one of the most ambitious goals a Master swimmer could ever aim for: compete in all eighteen events to earn the title of Iron Master. I kept telling myself that this was naturally the next step in my swimming adventure, for which I have already taken on crossings in open water, international meets and long distance events. And I wanted to understand why those who succeed in the endeavor feel like they are so special. I am aware of the fact that, given my current abilities, this is a dual challenge: on one end because I have to compete in events in which I have no experience and, on the other hand, because I have never swum those events, not even in lap swim. To say it like it is, for butterfly and backstroke, I had never competed in distances over 50 meters; in fact, in butterfly, I had never swum more than two consecutive laps. I motivate myself by saying that "to make your dreams come true, all you need is wish for them with all your heart."

I began my preparation for the Iron Master title by taking on the events with which I was familiar. Within three months, I competed in the 50, 100, 200, 400 and 1500 freestyle, leaving the 800-meter event for the spring. The interesting thing was that I was able to improve all my time and I even won the gold medal in the 50-meter freestyle event at the meet in Sondrio. Admittedly, there were only six swimmers in my category; however, it is also true that, in the end, I was the one to come out on top, rather than somebody else. In between so many freestyle events, I was able to squeeze in the 50-meter and 200-meter breaststroke (during the latter event, I began feeling ants in my wrists starting from the sixth lap), the 50-meter backstroke and the 100-meter individual medley. Then, in January, I participated in two meets that were very challenging for me...

I had always hated doing the backstroke: as I couldn't see where I was going, it often happened that I bumped my head against the wall at the end of the lane and my hands against the lane dividers. As if that weren't enough, I struggled to maintain a horizontal position because my legs kept dropping down, as if they were dragged down by a mysterious force. For these and other reasons, when the 100-meter backstroke event was approaching, I convinced myself that it would be fundamental to come up with a strategy. I entered the water and, as planned, I swam 50 meters slowly and 50 meters quickly. When I completed my event, I was satisfied because I succeeded in finishing the race without running out of breath, but also disappointed because I did not use up all my energy. For the time being, things worked out like that. An hour later, I returned to that same lane to compete in the 50-meter butterfly event. For this race, my challenge was all in my mind. Every time I thought of competing in a butterfly

event, I relived the horrible experience I had in Bergamo, two years earlier. What reassured me was the certainty that this time things would be different because since then I had not only swam a few hundred kilometers, but I also learned to breathe at every stroke, satisfying my hunger for oxygen that, after a few meters, closed out my lungs. I got this idea of using this breathing method by observing Michael Phelps during the World Swimming Championships. I told myself, "If he does it and he can still beat his opponents who breathe less frequently, why can't I?" At the start, I dove in and swam calmly, without feeling fatigued. When I arrived at the end of the second lap, I looked at my time and realized that it had dropped by four seconds. Only one detail left me hanging: once again I felt like I was swimming at the pace of a snail, almost as if I could not kick into a higher gear. I asked myself what I could do to increase my speed, but I didn't have time to find an answer: I had to begin preparing for the 200-meter butterfly event!

If I wanted to succeed in earning the title of Iron Master, I must complete the butterfly events, which were by far the hardest challenge in surpassing my limits. Maybe I had never fully mastered butterfly or maybe I got too jittery when I swam that stroke; the fact is that I dreaded swimming that stroke, even during practice. As my new challenge was approaching, I tried to seize the secrets of those who did the fly apparently without getting tired. For a long time, I observed the butterfly swimmers, but, as I realized that observing was not enough, I adopted a more direct approach, asking them a very simple question, "Can you explain how anyone can swim butterfly for eight laps consecutively?" I receive disappointing answers, such as, "You have to train a lot", "You must improve your technique," as well as some cryptic ones, "You have to stretch out your swim." In the meantime, time went by and I was still confused.

I went back to observing people under water, specifically targeting one of my teammates who did the fly just like a mermaid. I tried to imitate her harmonious body movements, but, besides a lot of splashing and some pulled muscles in my back, my progress was hardly noticeable. I reached the conclusion that the time I had left would not give me the possibility to learn anything other than what I already knew, so I chose to improve my endurance by attempting to complete the 200-meter swim in my solo practices. The first time that I tried swimming the entire distance, I drank endless amounts of water. The following times, I always completed the distance, although my times were way unsatisfactory. I didn't care about all that. I was especially concerned about the last of the eight laps I must complete in the race because, regardless of the pace I swam, it was devastating to try to complete the entire distance. If I missed just one thing during the competition, I would be forced to withdraw from the event...

For the first time from when I began competing, I was experiencing a feeling of tranquility. In some ways, this may seem paradoxical, considering that in a few minutes I would be competing in the 200-meter butterfly event; however, as my only expectation was to reach the end of the race, my heart felt as light as a feather. In this state of semi-tranquility, I enjoyed the wait together with the other swimmers from my heat, obviously heat 1, the slowest. The age of my "opponents" averaged around fifty years old, even if one of them had abundantly surpassed the seventy year mark. We quietly looked at each other and smiled.

There were no words to say at this time because we were all asking ourselves the same thing, "What on earth are we doing this for?" In the end, we are not professionals, but workers, parents or grandparents. It didn't matter because, in a few minutes, we would be in the water thinking about winning our own personal challenges.

Here we go. We were standing in front of the starting blocks. I took off my thermal shirt, put on my cap and goggles and then I began to mentally prepare myself. I climbed on the starting block. At the start signal, I let myself slide into the water, simulating a dive; then, I emerged after ten meters of underwater work, realizing that I successfully completed my entry as planned. Stretching out my stroke and feeling relaxed, I began to do the fly. I felt like I was moving a bit too quickly, so I slowed down and stretched out even more. The two swimmers on my sides leaped ahead of me, but I ignored them and took enjoyment in what I was doing. At the fourth lap, I felt like I still had all the energy in this world; I asked myself if I were swimming a little too slowly and, in response to that thought, I slightly increased my pace. Sixth lap: if math is not an opinion, I only had two laps left to go! I was impressed with myself. I maintained the same rhythm, but I didn't feel the same muscle block that came over me every time I swam this stroke. As my mind wandered on, I ended the race and reached the touch pad. My results were unforgiving: second to last in my age group. However, when I exited the pool, I was super-excited. I couldn't stop telling myself, "Hooray! I completed the 200-meter butterfly event!"

I began enjoying the 200-meter swims, so, after completing the butterfly race, I began training for the eight-lap backstroke event. Also in this case, I trained on Sunday mornings performing an infinite series of experiments: I swam on one side, swam using only legs and only arms. It was unbelievable, but true: my performance visibly improved. In the water, I was more relaxed and I stretched out my stroke; as I swam, I appeared taller than those who, although naturally well-endowed in terms of height, curled up like paper when they were in the water. My interest for this stroke, which was nil at the beginning, grew rapidly.

I later participated in Lombardy's Regional Champs and took on the 200-meter backstroke, feeling loose and tidy during my swim. I completed my race in a time with which I was satisfied and that, for a change, did not relegate me at the end of the rankings. At this point, I felt like I would like to double-check my progress so I again participated in the 50- and 100-meter backstroke events. My performances improved respectively by five and nine seconds. Now it was official: I had fallen in love with backstroke!

I had no problems taking on the 800-meter freestyle and the 100-meter breaststroke, events in which I had already participated in the past: I faced them without fears. Even in these cases I successfully set personal records, which surprised me and confirmed that I was on my way to improve my technique. The 100-meter butterfly and the 200-meter individual medley were completed without any hang-ups, leaving me with a sweet taste of victory when I went to record my times in my Excel spreadsheet.

It was now April. To complete my Iron Master, all I have left to do was complete my 400-meter individual medley. For this special occasion, I invited: my girlfriend with a camcorder (if things turned out for the worst... she would at least have one last memory of me), my buddies, friends and the essential assistance of the Lord. My suffering was mixed in with fun because I was to compete in a very competitive heat: in the middle lanes, a girl and I chased each other back and forth. We began behind everybody and ended up seizing first and second place in a final sprint that allowed her to prevail by only two tenths of a second. Once I was out of the water, and I was dressed, dried and relaxed, I turned back to look at the pool to enjoy in silence and intimacy the greatest swimming achievement of my life: earning the title of Iron Master!

Giuseppe is a Class 55 Master Swimmer. In 2001, on the day after he competed in the 1500meter freestyle event at Città di Castello and said goodbye to his friends with the sadness of someone who knows he has to be gone for a long period of time, he went to the hospital to undergo a bone marrow transplant. It's not his first time having to face such a tough challenge, considering that fifteen years earlier he had to fight and win his fight against the great disease. Anyhow, he knew that he had to prepare for one of the most difficult battles that a human being must ever face in his life. Next to him, always there to support him during his most difficult moments is a photo of Mother Teresa of Calcutta given to him by a dear friend. Therapies marked the years that followed, turning out to be devastating times, alternated with relapses in the disease. Regardless, when Giuseppe could, he went to train and participated in some meets, ignoring his doctors' advice to avoid any physical strain following his chemotherapy sessions. From this point of view, Giuseppe became a scientific case. His hospital stays continued; the isolation regimen was tough and, in his mind, his drive to dive back into the pool became ever greater. In a recurring dream, he envisioned himself as a young swimmer taking on a long-distance event in open waters. In the dream, he dove in and, shortly after, he saw his opponents disappear from sight. He was left all alone, swimming "in an atmosphere of surreal tranquility, wrapped up in bright and transparent light rays, lost in the haze of dreams" and he swam without experiencing any fatigue, stretching out his body and feeling relaxed. Without getting tired, he tried to reach the buoy in the distance, but, despite his efforts, he could not seem to get closer to it. When he finally reached the buoy, he was no longer a young man; he was his current age and his many friends surrounded him, complimenting him for his amazing achievement.

Being in a physical condition that made him experience reality as if it were a bit muffled, he decided that once he recovered from the disease, he would like to participate in open water competitions and, a bit for the joy of the challenge and a bit for keeping with the vow he made to Mother Teresa, he set his aims on completing the journey to earning the title of Iron Master. But when could he do all this? If he waited until the end of his treatment cycles, that moment may never arrive. And so he began to participate in open water competitions, despite his treatments were still ongoing. He competed in four intermediate-distance events, obtaining times that left him feeling very satisfied. Then, he began training for the Iron Master title, embarking on a journey made of practices and treatment, meets and treatment. The butterfly events were the toughest and most challenging races for him, but he certainly did not give up when faced with those: he fought, overcame his challenges and completed all eighteen events, earning his Iron Master title. His love for swimming, together with therapy and joy of living, has so far given him, as he himself loves to say, twenty years of life.

ANALYSIS – Continuous improvement

No matter how much you may be surrounded by other people, when you swim you are alone with yourself, in touch with your thoughts and feelings. While in this condition, it is unavoidable that you mainly attribute your victories to the strength of your arms and legs, although supported by the important work of your coach. So it happens that, when you succeed in completing an especially challenging swimming event, to obtain a certain swim time you wished for, or simply to swim a stroke especially well, you think of yourself as the undisputed protagonist of that success. For this reason, every time you succeed, you feel grown up, more confident in your abilities and ready to bet that you can do even better. It is a virtuous circle that makes you gain maturity, both as an athlete and a human being.

Your small successes in sports, making you understand the winning effect of putting forth an effort, perseverance and determination, in everyday life, can give you an extra gear. Before I began practicing sports, the rhythm of my life was comparable to that of city traffic at rush hour. My progress was limited and achieved only at the high expense of stress and an endless fight against others. Then I began swimming and my mental growth took the freeway to success, where progress is appreciated for its long reach.

When I grasped what had happened to me, I wanted to check if others also felt the same way. I realized that not everyone progresses systematically because, for the most part, those who achieve something good convince themselves that they can't do better, despite the enormous potential at their disposal. Why? The reasons may be partly understood by considering what I shared in the previous pages as well as partly connected to the lack of a method. The method, together with a positive approach and adult reactions is what enabled me to improve with continuity.

When I decided to transcribe my approach, I realized that I hadn't invented anything new. I understood that, my profession on one hand and my readings on swimming on the other led me to interiorize a system already written by others. I only had to absorb those principles and let my subconscious re-elaborate everything. Then, without even being aware of it, I began using the "amalgam," reaching the successes that you read about in these pages.

So, you may already be familiar with what I am proposing. At any rate, you will find my process interesting because it is adapted to the world of swimming. If you are a master athlete who uses the art of making do, you know that what you are about to read is the way to take the highway to success…

1. DECIDING TO IMPROVE

Everything starts with you deciding to improve a specific situation. Your making that decision is essential because that is what motivates your actions, providing encouragement.

The stronger is your decision, the farther your motivation will take you. But how do you take a motivating decision?

At the base of it all there is always an intense emotion that you may have experienced personally living through an event or merely as a spectator.

Sometimes it is something you do to generate that emotion which, pleasant or not, pushes you to change things. For example, it may have happened to you when you saw the house you wanted to live in and, walking around its rooms you had the strong feeling that you were at ease, so, despite the high sale or rental price, you decided that you would have made sacrifices to live there. Alternatively, you may have felt a motivating emotion when you discovered that you gained weight and, at that point, although it may have been difficult, you started a diet and even began to run to burn off your excess weight.

Other times, all you need is learning the story of a friend to feel a motivating emotion and decide to follow your friend's example. Try to remember how you chose to follow your path in school: did you discover everything by yourself or did you listen to the stories of someone you knew who, by telling you stories, made you feel emotions to the point that you saw yourself earning that diploma? Or even yet, try to remember how you chose your car. A friend or a salesperson may have described the features of that vehicle: when you set in it to test-drive it, you felt like this car was for you, so you signed your name on the loan paper-work and off you went with your new hot rod.

There is something else to it, too: as intensely as you may feel something, emotions are just the trigger; after the initial stages, in order for your motivation to continue to burn, you need to fuel it with more firewood, that is to say a series of elements that can help you strengthen the good choice you made. Let's get back to the example of the house. When you located the house that you liked, you surely did one thing: you focused on the positive features that supported your choice and downplayed or eliminated those details that may have made you change your mind. For example, you repeatedly remarked, "ah, this dining room is so large" (the reinforcement), conveniently redefining the noisy traffic as something that may be overcome with double pane windows (reducing the negative aspect).

An emotion, the same emotion, may produce a decision toward a positive change (improving something) or a negative one (quitting). Seeing a protruding waistline, which for some is so unbearable to drive them to take action may make you say, "Oh well, who cares about diets and health! I am going to continue eating whatever I want since the situation is way beyond repair... in the end, you only live once!" This means that choosing to follow one path, rather than another is something that depends on a reaction that is triggered within you, as I had the opportunity to recount in Chapter 5. A loser's reaction pushes you to let go, give up and, in some cases, hold grudges against those who succeed.

On the other hand, a winner's reaction pushes you to take decisions that drive positive change, make you put forth a higher effort and to find a solution to change and improve your current situation...

I have always wanted to swim the 50-meter freestyle event in less than thirty seconds. After my time dropped two seconds below my first seed time ever, for two years I always came fractions of a second close to twenty-nine seconds. This was not the result of me avoiding trying new things: I tried to jump the starting gun, running the risk of a false start; I tried swimming almost without breathing; I

even increased the number of my arm strokes, thinking that it would help me glide better over the water, but nothing seemed to work: I couldn't seem to drop below that time. One day, it so happened that two of my teammates who wished to achieve the same goal, succeeded. I remember feeling a very strong emotion when I heard the news; I felt it in my gut and it felt half way between happiness for them and sadness for me. It only lasted a few moments and that's all it took for me to feel a shiver run from my head to my feet, which drove me to say, "If they made it, I can make it, too." A hypnosis section would not have worked better. Avoiding all excuses, my body began to give even more energy during practice. On the other hand, my mind began elaborating unprecedented solutions, making me note in the videos of my meets a detail that I had never noticed before: the rolling motion of my head during the most excited phases of my sprint. Needless to say that such a movement contributed only to make me lose the proper posture, creating an unavoidable drag. As I recovered from my shock, I made up some exercises that allowed me to focus on my head.

A few months later, everything happened with extreme naturalness. At the Brescia Brixia Invitational, in a fifty-meter pool, I dove in and ended the event with a time of 29.26 seconds! My joy was uncontainable. Then, as if I had done the easiest thing in the world, it came natural for me to think, "...twenty-eight seconds are not that far, after all!"

Take my word for it. To make an objective more effective, write it down on SMART paper, as I explained in Chapter 6. Once you have defined it, you can visualize it; and, if you visualize it, your mind can focus your energy and enable you to give decidedly higher level performances.

2. OBSERVATION

If you have committed to paper your decision to improve, then you focused on a couple of elements on which you wish your attention. Before you begin to act, you must first gather information that will be useful to plan the specific steps that will lead you from where you currently are to where you want to be. How can you prepare for this journey? Watch the others!

Choose two swimmers to follow: one must be a professional and the other should be someone around you, slightly better than you. You'll need the double reference to set your first step as well as the ideal objective on which to set your aims. It's a little like, if you were in Milan, you would take the decision to go to Florence (your improvement objective). At that point, you would have to mark the location of Florence on the map, find Lodi (that someone slightly better than you) as well as the location of Rome (the performance of the professional swimmer, who swims way better than your objective, indicating the ideal trajectory). Remember that the farther you set your first point of reference, the higher is the risk of getting lost; conversely, the closer it is, the more direct and immediate your path will be.

What exactly do I mean by watching the others? First of all, observe what they do in terms of movement, aiming at seizing those few details that you wish to copy. When you are in the water, don't just think of swimming your way, but try to watch those better than you to try to understand how they do some things. Stop at the edge of the pool, immerse your head under water holding your breath and memorize the positions of their bodies in the crucial moments of their swim. Let me give you an example. If your problem is that you don't bend your elbow well during the underwater phase of your freestyle (pull phase), then look closely when the swimmer you are watching bends his forearm. Does this take place when his hand enters the water or when it passes by his eyes? Is his thumb facing upward or is it turned a different way? Try to seize as many details as you can so that you can reproduce what you just watched. When you transition from theory to practice, don't limit yourself to a few tries. Try to complete a good number of repetitions; then, when you think that you have arrived at your destination, move your attention to the feelings you experience and memorize them because those are your personal references that will allow you to repeat that movement over time. Feelings are a bit like sewing pins: they temporarily fasten the clothes on your body before the final sewing makes them a permanent fit.

In regards to using a professional as a reference, you can view videos of him on the internet. Once you find a video from an angle that you like, pause the video to study the details that illustrate a specific item on which you wish to zero-in; then recreate that stance as soon as you have a chance to practice. If you use determination, constancy and patience, while always staying alert with what you do, even when you are tired or you realize that you are falling behind compared to the others, within a few weeks you will realize how your technique will significantly improve, taking you always closer to your "Florence." But that's not all.

Copying others also means sharing their state of mind. And there is a simple way to do that: use their words. All this is based on the principle of neurolinguistic connections, which I mentioned in Chapter 5. Listen to what other swimmers say. Pay attention to the words and metaphors they use. It has happened to me to gather very precious information on their mindset. Here are some examples: "I can turn quickly because, when I touch the wall, I think of it as burning as hot coals;" "When I crouch down on the starting block, I load up like a spring, so at the start signal, it's easy for me to jump in like a grasshopper;" "Every arm stroke feels like it's full of water;" "When I dive in, I visualize a hole in the water; then I try to put my arms, head, pelvis and feet in that hole." Here and there, I found some expressions quite funny; then, I tried repeating them in the same settings and the end result was that I improved my performance from the first try!

In order to gather useful information to draft your map, read books, stories, blogs and sites about swimming. In addition to learning all types of experiences, you can run into exciting tales that may renew your motivation and drive. That happened to me when I read Mark Spitz's biography. I knew that Olympic champions are constantly searching for technical details to improve; what I didn't know was that someone had the opportunity to scientifically prove that he swam the perfect swim...

In 1990, eighteen years after his memorably winning seven gold medals at the Munich Olympics, Mark Spitz was again in the spotlight. Besides being past 41 years of age, he announced his comeback to competitive swimming to attempt to qualify for the 1992 Olympic Games in Barcelona. A Japanese documentary maker got the scoop and set up an efficiency test for Mark to take at the Colorado Springs sports center. All Mark had to do was immerse himself in an artificial channel and swim. The water was moved by a motor, which, similarly to a treadmill, may be set to any speed. A computer system was to capture 3D images, through which it could define the rate of efficiency of the swim.

Mark entered the tube and did the butterfly. At first, he found it a bit difficult to keep up with the set speed, also because it was that of the best performance in the world, which was much faster than the one with which Mark had won the Olympic games years earlier. After a few moments of feeling out of breath, Mark picked up the rhythm and maintained it for the required amount of time. At the end of the test, the computer processed the captured images, producing a graph made of two lines: one indicating the potential performance for the subject and the other indicating his current level. This system had been used to measure the performance of various world swimmers. The technicians grabbed Mark's results and they were startled by what they saw: for the first time ever, the lines of the ideal and real seem almost entirely overlapping! Mark Spitz's secret was therefore revealed: unlike the others, he could fully express his potential.

3. ACTION

At this point, you are holding the map showing the directions from your first step to the final objective. It is time to switch to action and, through practice, fix those details that you decided to improve. In this phase, you will need two tools: one is your work program and the other is a list of smaller objectives.

The workout schedule is an outline of exercises whose ultimate goal is to pick up the elements observed in the swim. The more you vary your exercises, the more pins you will put on your clothes and more precise your final seams will be. This happens because by attempting the right movement in various situations, you detect more feeling around your muscles contracting and your body gliding through the water. Make up your own exercises or borrow them from websites or swim manuals.

On the other hand, the minor objectives serve the purpose

of giving a specific goal to every single practice. Let me explain. Every time you enter the water, you must set a goal, even though it may just be a simple one. If you are trying to improve lateral breathing on your left side because you just can't breathe as well as on the right side, besides completing a series of targeted exercise, try to define an incremental objective. For example, in an early session, set the goal to breathe on the left side for at least twenty laps; the following time, increase that to twenty-one laps, then twenty-two and so on. This allows you to quantify your improvement, ensuring, at the same time, a progressive commitment toward reaching your goal.

Method and self-discipline make up the winning combination to get away from the mold of things that are always done the way they have always been done, enabling you to follow the path to improvement. Obviously, don't ever forget to add a good dose of curiosity...

I felt immense joy and satisfaction when I completed my first Iron Master. Never in my life had I ever felt as good and brave in a sport; above all, I would have never through of being able to do something like that. I had acquired the awareness that, in specific circumstances, every single drop of my sweat could yield big dividends. Taking the decision of repeating the Iron Master was already set in stone from the beginning. In the end, I was familiar with the procedure. In fact, I "only" had to follow the same path as before, being careful not to repeat the same mistakes as in the past, such as showing up for the 200-meter butterfly event with the pressing fear of not making it. Therefore, I consciously decided to change my technique so I could fluidly swim eight laps without having to turn to prayer. The next step was to observe the videos of elite competitions and my better teammates swim. I felt like that

wasn't enough so I asked Claudia to take a video of me swimming to obtain objective data on my technique. Good heavens, what an eye-opener that was! When I looked over the video, for a moment I thought I should quit swimming that stroke altogether: instead of swimming harmoniously, I just alternated slapping arms and legs in between enormous useless pauses. The first thing to do was fix my synchronism.

Examining the champion's competitions, I had noticed how the push begins from the swimmer's legs, rather than his arms, so I had to dedicate time to enhancing the sensibility of my legs. I remembered having read somewhere that using fins may turn out to be a decisive factor in nailing the proper kicking technique, so I bought a pair of fins. I made up a series of exercises to gather bullets to "check off" by tapping into all my creativity to even make it fun to swim two thousand meters by only using my feet. The minor objectives obviously involved the consecutive meters of fluid swim, which I had to achieve before I could let it fall apart as a result of fatigue.

Do you know what brought me to all that? Within a few months, I succeeded in improving the time in my 50-meter butterfly event, taking my personal record from thirty-nine to thirty-five seconds! And that's not all, considering that I was able to drop thirty seconds in my 200-meter butterfly event!

4. ANALYS RESULTS

After having acted in the action phase, if you formulated your objective in a SMART way (see Chapter 6), when the defined time expires, it will be time to evaluate if the results you obtained are in line (or not) with your objectives: if you have reached Florence, as you wished to do, or did you end up in Bologna, Genoa or Trieste? Pay attention to one thing:

in this phase it is fundamentally important to never use the word, "failure" to comment on a result different from what you expected. The reason behind this, as I had a chance to tell you, is that some words have the only result of putting you in a very unproductive state of mind, which sooner or later will lead you to believe that the best way to win a challenge is to let someone else do it. Therefore, whether you reached your goal or ended up somewhere else, analyze your results with curiosity and neutrality. Did you reach Florence, as you wished? Make note of the strategies that have worked for you so that you can use them again in other occasions. Did you end up somewhere else? Mark the turns you missed, so that, in the future, you can avoid making the same mistakes.

I know that it is hard to push back disappointment when you have worked long and hard and you haven't been able to improve: I have been there many times. For this reason, I came up with my own personal strategy that allows me to get over "unpredictable results." This is it: ten minutes of complaining, then look to the future and get back to work with more joy and enthusiasm then before. Reacting as an adult may be helpful, but, even more importantly, keep one thing in mind:

"True growth is not achieved by reaching your destination, but rather by enjoying the journey."

EMOTION
Now I know why it's called Iron Master

For many, this may be a competition, a game or one of many ways to practice a sport, but for others, and I know what I am saying, completing the Iron Master means winning a challenge against yourself. For those who, like me, have entered the world of swimming from the back door, at the end of this nice trip, I felt grown up. Competition after competition, I had the opportunity to bring down the wall of limits that, for a long time, made me believe that I was not capable. Milestone after milestone, I was able to lift my chin, gaze upon the horizon and surprisingly realize how many of my goals were attainable. After competing in all eighteen events, a new world lay ahead of me and, looking at that new world almost makes my heart skip a beat. And that heart is now as strong as iron and it no longer has any fears: not of being last in the standings, not of the events in which I have never competed and not to look bad. I chose to leave those types of fears for the hearts of those who prefer sitting there, looking on and criticizing, rather that daring to take on and attempting the journey.

I decided to take a step forward to find for myself all my limits, without hiding or justifying any of them.

I decided to grow up and push myself farther, hanging on with all my strength to that edge that is my passion for swimming.

I have decided to prove to myself, but also others, that limits are set to be surpassed.

Today, with unique and intense satisfaction, I can say that…I now understand why they call it Iron Master: because I too am an Iron Master now.

EXERCISE

Think of an aspect you need to improve, whatever it may be. Take time in selecting it because you must...
DECIDE TO IMPROVE

_____

_____

_____

OBSERVE
Now write how you will gather the information you need to make that improvement.

_____

_____

_____

ACT
Return to this page once you obtain the information you need and write on the lines below the actions that you will undertake to produce the desired results (plan specific exercises and goals).

_____

_____

_____

ANALIZE RESULTS
Now it's time to go over your results. Did you reach your destination or did you find a way not to arrive where you wanted to be?

_____

_____

_____

CHAPTER 10: OTHER CHALLENGES

EXPERIENCE – Love for the sport

Cap, goggles and FIN membership card: yes, I definitely had everything, including that unavoidable emotion that always takes over me right before a meet. Years had passed since I had first set foot on a starting block; however, even after so much time, nothing had changed inside me: a moment before diving in, my heart started beating out of control, my breathing changed to quick short breaths and, to avoid being taken over by my emotions, I forced myself to maintain upright posture and controlled ventilation. Everything was just like it was thirty-four years ago, when I first debuted in the Masters swimming competitions and I swam that unforgettable 100-meter breaststroke, including getting disqualified. Today, at the age of seventy-five, I continued to experience the world of swimming as if I were exploring it for my first time. I looked around and, for a moment, my eyes lingered on other swimmers of my age, those who were also blessed with good health and wrinkly skin, although their pores were filled with passion and desire to feel emotions. I felt lucky and, at the same time, worthy of what had happened to me, because every time that I had to take an important decision in life, I had always considered my alternatives, thinking of where each decision would lead compared to my vision of personal fulfillment.

It is truly important for you to know early on what you want from life because otherwise you run the risk of arriving to the end of your days without knowing where you ended up or if you successfully achieved what you had set out to do. And to know that, you must sit there, think, wish and then write it down. That is exactly what I had done many years earlier: I had taken pen and paper and, with abundant details, I had described what my life would be like, someday. Today, I still held on to those yellowed papers, which contain sentences like, "...and happy and smiling, I am sitting in a nice house with a yard, welcoming and well maintained. I am surrounded by my loved ones; they also are happy and smiling. The crystal hutch set in the middle of the living room displays all the trophies and medals that I won over the years. At first glance, it looks like they must belong to at least ten different people!"

The following pages clearly show the intermediate steps that progressively allowed me to get to this point. I remembered: writing those papers was a long and laborious exercise because I had to decide what was important for me, excluding less relevant things so that I could head directly to what would placate me on the day I evaluated the quality of my journey through this world. I received the motivation to do something like that from a motivational book and, exactly as I had read, I first visualized what I wanted to achieve; then I touched it, sniffed it, tasted it and lived it in a typical day of my future life. This was an amazing technique to provide your brain with an experience and a very precise point of reference to help you make choices. Thinking back on it, I thanked heaven for being able to plan my future so minutely because now that I admired it, I felt privileged. Let me be clear: things did not always go well for me. I too had my moments of suffering, struggling and falls to pick myself up. There is no such thing as a perfect life without problems, glitches, difficulties or challenges to be overcome, but if you are willing to accept the idea that, along your way, you may encounter challenges and unexpected events of any type; then you are also willing to accept the rule that, "There's always a price to pay." And, at that point, you will face everything with courage and make your choices with serenity, without ever regretting to have taken one path rather than another. My passion for swimming led me to make choices and to give up some things, too. I wanted to dedicate time to sport, taking some away from other things, well aware of the reasons why I was doing what I was doing. So I resisted the losers' voices that played in my head and I ignored those who, not understanding me all the way, disapproved by using phrases like, "You know, nobody can give you back the time you spent swimming back and forth in the pool! Oh well, it's your life..." Right, it's my life, and that's the only truth in that statement. I always followed my path, carefully listening only to my dear ones, thanks to which I was able to build a solid balance between time spent together and time dedicated to my sport.

Today, I could not be more satisfied. I would like to shout it out to the four winds and, in a certain way, it was exactly what I was quietly doing, sitting here among the elderly swimmers of my age, waiting for my 800-

meter freestyle event of the 2048 Italian Masters Championships. Even they had a unique story to tell and every one of them deserved a book such as this one. For example, Giovanni, the guy sitting next to me, was at his twentieth Championship. Claudio, sitting two rows ahead of us as he was in a slightly slower heat, was sixty-five years old and this was his first time participating in a national competition. He had just recently discovered master's level swimming, although he had been keeping in shape by swimming laps for ten years. He was proud of what he was about to do: you could see it in his shimmering eyes. Then there was Andrea, the most laid back of them all and certainly not because he was sixty-nine years old; he would soon transition to the Master 80 category. He simply loved concentrating on what he needed to do as he intended to impress his loved ones, who had come to watch him. He funnily noted that, instead of him sitting on the bleachers, those sitting there were his children, grandchildren and even a young great-grandson!

I listened to everybody with extreme interest, day-dreaming and getting excited, at the same time. Then, I looked around and realized that, despite my age, the scenario was always the same: the people wearing bathing suits belong to different generations and have varying swimming abilities, but they all share the same immense passion.

Here we go: they were calling my name; it was my turn. In a few moments, I would begin my race and do what I had always done: dive in, swim and put all my heart, mind and soul in it until I couldn't bear it anymore, knowing full well that, after the effort, the suffering, the mind haze and muscle predicaments, once I was outside the pool, I would feel happy and filled by this indescribable joy that only a sports lover has the privilege to experience, that something that makes you say every time, "This is it: this is why I make so many sacrifices! And I can't wait to do it again!"

Maybe the day I will read over the above lines I will smile thinking of how good I was at imagining what I would be like at seventy-five. Maybe I will realize even more the power of the tool with which I equipped myself, which, in practical terms, took only the commitment of a few days to decide what to do in life and then write it on some sheets of paper as accurately as possible. With little effort, I was able to obtain a mental navigator that gave me the path to follow, automatically recalculating directions in case that, due to the inevitable events of life, I may happen to take the wrong turn.

Today, I live like this, relying on the map that I wrote, sure that I am approaching as much as possible the destination that I chose. The biggest advantage is that I can relax and enjoy every moment of this wonderful journey, which will represent the path of my life...

October 26, 7:30 AM. I was driving my car, traveling toward my first meet of the season, which was traditionally held in the isolated but pretty location in Verolanuova. I was driving, trying to untangle thousands of thoughts spinning around in my head, including expectations to succeed and correct strategies to put me in condition to produce those results. I mentally prepared myself to do well in the 50-meter backstroke event, a stroke that I felt like I had improved with the technical workouts I had done over the summer and I even prepared myself to improve my 50-meter freestyle, not so much aiming for my absolute record, but to improve my best time from last year. This is one of the many ways to make me motivated at the beginning of the season, when the physical condition I just mentioned does not allow for amazing performances.

Then I thought of Claudia, who was sitting here next to me. It was not unusual for her to travel with me to meets. Since we had started dating, about one and one-half years ago, she hadn't missed a meet. However, this time... well, this time it was her turn! After attending a swim course and acquiring a little technique in other strokes, she decided to experience competitive swimming, reserving the right to quit in case she found out that she didn't like it.

When I met her, although she had never signed up for swim classes in her life, in the summer, she usually swam one hundred laps each and every day all rigorously in freestyle or flutter kick. I remember I was impressed by how much she swam for the sole purpose of staying in shape. Once we became closer, I had asked her, "Why don't you join the master's swimming program with us? When I started, I had one-fourth of your endurance!" and she had answered, "What for? I only know how to swim freestyle; I would have to learn the other strokes first." She surely did. She took the beginner-advanced course for one year, with her instructors incredulously watching her double the other swimmers in freestyle and then sink when trying to do the breaststroke and the backstroke, but now, here she was. If I thought of all the times I had to explain the breaststroke kick, it seemed impossible that I hadn't eaten my goggles out of desperation, hearing her say for the umpteenth time, "...I can't see my legs; how can I understand what I have to do and how to do it? I can't, I can't..." But then, it was dancing that had caused her such damage: ballerinas learn to perform their movements spending their entire time in front of the mirror and this was the result! The incredible thing is that, once she learned the correct movement, she perfected it in very little time, gaining propulsion far superior to mine in her lower extremities.

I said, "We are almost at Verolanuova," waking her up from her unavoidable car-ride nap. "Warm up begins at 8 AM sharp. Do not be startled if, before the beginning of the meet, the pool will feel like a tuna net. If it all goes well, you may complete a few hundred meters together with half a thousand people." As if she didn't hear me, she answered, "I can't wait to have some Ginseng coffee." I smiled. Then, acting like those who have infinite experience, I stroked her hair, arranging it behind her ear and said, "Honey, have you looked around you? We are in the country, surrounded by the smell of cows, horses or God only knows what this natural manure smell is. It is simply a miracle that this area even has a swimming pool...well, in this setting do you really think that we'll find a bar? And what else would you like... a croissant? Ha, ha. You are so cute."

We arrived at the swimming pool at 7:55. We walked by the large windows of the sports center to reach the entrance. Claudia looked at me and, laughing whole-heartedly, she said, "Well, look, there's a bar! They even make ginseng coffee and they have a pile of steaming croissants. Would you like one?"

I don't know if it was the love she feels for me or the love that swimming arises in the people who practice it; the fact is that Claudia began enjoying competing and noticing that, already from the second year of masters swimming, your times can drop. She loves swimming, and, even more so, she adores competing and chasing one improvement after another. It's not by chance that we plan our vacations to spend time in places where the sea is crystal clear. It's not by chance that what we enjoy most about being in salt water is to get away from the shore and swim for hours surrounded by schools of minnows. It's not even by chance that our romance begun after an outing to Lake Como, that I asked her to marry me on the lake and that we also celebrated our wedding there.

I found love at the swimming pool. At the pool, I also made many friends. Among the many wonderful people I had the pleasure of meeting is one that, more than anyone, has touched my heart. It's my dear friend Alberto. Alberto is a wonderful person. I met him a couple of years ago, when he joined our masters swim team. Alberto and I hit it off right away, and we immediately became friends for no specific reason. Maybe I saw myself in him or it seemed nice to imagine that I was like him because he is always smiling, nice, positive and full of energy. I don't know anybody who hasn't made friends with Alberto. He never shows off about anything; he is always easy going and feels at ease with everybody, as if he was a wise man who took vows to contemplate the world. Yet, inside of him, he has a hurricane that pushes him to achieve the most incredible challenges, challenges that, with a great degree of simplification, I tried to translate through my writing that you can read in the "Emotion" section of this chapter.

At the pool, I met friends like Alberto, but also rivals with which I shared some healthy competition. When it happens that you compete in a heat with one of your mates and rivals, the emotions you feel are amplified. The moments that precede the departure are indescribable: you can feel the adrenaline pumping, your heart beating and a feeling an almost unique energy. And all this takes place with nothing concrete being up for grabs. The only satisfaction we try to get is to arrive before the others, knowing full well that, no matter what the outcome is, in the end we will be complementing and thanking each other for what we shared...

I will never forget the day in which I realized I had become a good swimmer. It took patience, perseverance and ease; then it happened. I remember that day being very special: the most extraordinary day of my sports adventure. He was the best swimmer on the team: I always saw him train in the "Tsunami" lane, the one reserved for the team's best swimmers. I, on the other hand, swam in the lane of the inadequate, and I stood there to admire such strength, excellence and endurance. At the time, he was fighting to drop below one minute in the 100-meter freestyle event, training with seriousness and determination, while I struggled quite a bit to drop below one minute and twenty seconds. In swimming, such difference is an abyss and a little like seeing motorcycle champion Valentino Rossi riding by, and then, twenty seconds later, seeing one of your friends riding a moped. I never thought that my swim times could approach his, so how could I ever dream of beating him? In a masters' meet, just to mention one, we found out that we had signed up for the same events. One of the events we had in common was the 50-meter back-stroke and, as we were in the same age group, we found ourselves in the same scoreboard: I came in last with a finals time of forty-nine seconds; he placed well finishing the race in thirty-seven seconds. The backstroke was a stroke that I always hated and never understood. Then things changed. And one day it happened.

That Sunday, during that meet, despite our respective personal records were at least ten seconds apart, we ended up in the same 200-meter backstroke event, which neither of us looked forward to swim. I, competing in this event for the third time, knew that he, combative as few, would never concede the victory to one who was half his size and hadn't participated in competitive swimming in his youth. However, that day, during that meet, what everyone least expected just happened. It so happened that I, swimming at the best of my ability, concentrating exclusively on my swim, on being light as a feather and fast as a torpedo, moving my hands in water in a determined yet precise way, after eight never-ending laps swum bearing a burning sensation of the muscles stressed to the max and tremendous panting, touched the pad one second before my teammate, with a finals time of 2 minutes and 57 seconds and improving my personal record by as much as ten seconds.

That day -I still remember it with incredible clarity- I enjoyed the sweetest taste that sport can offer: that of the immense satisfaction of a result produced by mental strength.

That day, I was able to surpass all the false beliefs that had long been spinning in my head. And this is the reasons why a few months later I again succeeded in beating him again, even in the event we are best at: the 50-meter freestyle in a long distance pool, where only the fastest can win. This all happened because that day, during that backstroke event, I realized that I had finally become... a *good swimmer*.

ANALYSIS – Proud of yourself

Swimming is a tough sport. You spend hours upon hours at the pool with your head under water, speaking to yourself, only to try to drop your time by a few fractions of a second. This happens at all levels: both in competitive swimming, which involves all those who dream of disputing the Olympics and in master's level swimming, whose participants see swimming as way to win personal challenges. For everyone, the formula is always the same: results = commitment x training. Nothing comes free; if you want to reach your objectives, you must make a commitment, work hard at it, do your best and be assured that your victories will not be long in coming. But watch out for external assaults. If you read the biographies of great champions or listen to the statements of those who succeeded in doing something extraordinary, you will realize that around you there may be feelings of envy. Often times, those people who have always considered you a clumsy one loathe what you can do: they refuse to accept that you have evolved; they prevent you from moving forward and they will even trip you. Other times, those feeling envious toward you are those who cannot match your results, so they try to make you drop one level playing all sorts of mind games...

In the days before the 100-meter butterfly final event at the 2008 Beijing Olympic Games, Milorad Cavic, a Serbian swimmer, released a series of interviews to newspapers arguing that it would be nice to go down in history as the one who took away one of the eight gold medals that Michael Phelps needed to become the first to have won that many during the same Olympics. As you may know, in the end, Michael Phelps did win eight medals, surpassing the previous endeavor by Mark Spitz, who, in 1972, had won seven. However, before he could do that, Michael had to withstand even a second attack by Milorad. Right at the edge of the pool, a moment before the initial dive, the Serbian swimmer, after having exchanged glances with his adversary, stood there and continued staring at Phelps in a weak attempt to intimidate him.

The same thing happened the following year. During the 2009 World Swimming Championships in Rome, again before the 100-meter butterfly event, Cavic showed up with the flag of the Roma soccer team in order to obtain a louder cheer than what his opponent would get. Then, again, in front of the starting blocks, instead of looking down his lane, even in a more theatrical way that before, Cavic turned to stare at him like a dog; however, Michael easily ignored that. What was the outcome? Phelps won, confirming not only that he was the fastest, but also that he was the only one to possess the mental strength of a true champion.

Do not pay attention to those who, seeing you become good, try to question your results. Do not fight them, but limit yourself to do what you love to do with passion. With your excellent effort in commitment and tolerance, one day you will succeed in conquering them, too. In the most difficult moments, make an effort to remember that it is not within your possibilities to decide the thought of others, thus it is useless to worry about it. On the other hand, what you decided to do is to enjoy what you do.

Swimming teaches the value of commitment because without commitment nobody is capable of achieving any result. If you don't train, you can't expect to always be the fastest, to improve or grow. Water is a strict, unquestionable judge, which seizes your lack of preparation and, without sugarcoating it, transmits the feeling of being a stranger. The stopwatch is its inseparable ally: it measures you and coldly places you in front of reality.

Swimming is an individual sport. It continuously provides contact with oneself, with body and mind. If you succeed in bringing together the two parts and connect them with each other through your spirit, then you will be in the conditions not only to succeed but also to complete endeavors that immediately appear ridiculous…

Eric is a swimming champion. He was born in Georgia, USA. When he was 25 years old, he had everything a swimmer could dream of: exceptional results, excellent shape and the possibility to qualify for the Olympics. Eric was a step away from crowning his dream. He had to do one last tryout in the trials to earn a spot in the team for his country, next to the great Michael Phelps, whom everyone was talking about. The

trials, held one month before the Games, are used in America to select the swimmers who will participate in the Olympics. The top two selectees for each event are picked to participate in individual competitions and relay finals; those who placed high were slated to participate in the preliminary phases; while the rest stayed home to cheer in front of their television sets.

When Eric climbed on the starting block for the 200-meter breaststroke trials, he was no longer the carefree boy he had been a few weeks earlier: he was less concentrated, less serene and more vulnerable. Something very heavy and bothersome was weighing on his mind and this took away from his energy and focus. In his mind, he continued to hear the words he heard last week, words that sounded as a threat: "You have a testicular cancer." When you hear something like that, your head immediately feels empty and you feel lost as if you were inside an enormous white room with no windows and in which you only see a container as large as a box of matches, filled only with one thought: your disease. In these conditions, Eric awaited the start signal for the race that he did not want to pass up. He dove in, swam and won a spot to participate in the Beijing Olympic Games. His doctors give him the go-ahead and he participated in the Olympics, rescheduling his cancer surgery to after the sports event. Eric held the bitter secret in his heart until one night during the Olympics he shared it with his roommates. He returned home from the Olympic Games, having missed his qualification for the finals by only thirteen hundreds of a second and a very respectable personal record.

At this point, the hardest challenge began: undergo surgery and hope to win his fight against the bad disease. Three weeks after surgery, the doctors declared him cancer-free and Eric was reborn. He dedicated his talents to the Lance Armstrong (famous cyclist and cancer survivor, who won the Tour de France several times, years earlier) foundation, telling his story and returning to train for the World Championships.

At the trials, held in Indianapolis, he became the second American to swim the 100-meter breaststroke event in under one minute. He also earned a qualification for the 200-meter breaststroke and the 200-meter individual medley. To reward him for his performance, with great surprise, was a very special person: the doctor who had helped him to win his hardest challenge. Eric's father was also there. At the same age as his son, Eric's father had fought and survived lung cancer. The rest is history. So Eric participated as a protagonist in the World Swimming Championship of Rome, winning a silver medal in the 200-meter breaststroke (one hundredth of a second away from the gold), a bronze medal in the 200-meter individual medley and a gold medal and world record in the 4x100 mixed relay, together with his teammates Phelps, Peirsol and Walters.

As he himself stated, "Success is not defined by the wins you get, but by the obstacles you overcome."

If you practice a sport by setting goals, you know full well the pleasure one feels when you achieve them. A sense of fulfillment takes over your mind and body and, although this may momentarily placate your wish to act, after a few hours you will find yourself going back to dreaming something new to create. And dreaming is a feature that characterizes the unreasonable human being, who is not content with reality, but tries in every way to adapt reality to his own wishes.

If what you are reading seems strange or distant from your lifestyle, just know that you always have the ability to learn.

Just call out the child inside you, that part of your personality who knows what it means to dream and desire, but also try and create. That is because children do so following their natural predisposition. Try to ask a child what he wants to do when he grows up and he will tell you the most incredible dreams, using the most natural and certain tone in this world. And this is the secret to always remain young and active: continue to set goals, projects and dreams, just like children...

2009 was the year of Strait of Messina crossings. Within a few days, two children, an eleven-year-old girl and an eight-year-old boy made the news for having completed the challenge. The girl swam the strait in 41 minutes and the boy, who set the record as the youngest person ever to make the crossing, did so in 58 minutes. When interviewed by numerous journalists, they both expressed their joy with candor typical of their age. They used expressions like, "It seemed impossible, but I did it," or they may be already thinking of the future, "My next goal is the Strait of Gibraltar!"

Those who looked these children in the eyes realized that what glimmered inside them was not that light typical of those adults who are satisfied for having done something important, but rather the satisfaction of someone who succeeded in making the dream he held in his heart come true. Nothing and nobody can keep you from dreaming. Nothing and nobody can keep you from making your dreams come true. And although the outcome may not turn out to be what we expect, nothing and nobody can take away the pleasure of having tried. This is sports: dream of achieving something, apply yourself with passion and commitment and then get excited when you challenge yourself. The only outcome that really counts is: feeling proud of yourself always and no matter what…

I didn't think it could happen, but it has. I competed strongly believing in my improvement; I arrived thinking I had succeeded but, on the other hand…on the other hand, reality is different. The stopwatch says that my times have worsened, that my performance has gone back to that of 2 years ago and that, this time, I didn't have the pleasure of being pleasantly surprised with myself. I am perplexed. For a moment, I was tempted by delusion; then I said to myself, "What will I benefit from feeling defeated? Will it be good for me to feel sorry for myself? What will that solve?" I took a deep breath and examined differences and analogies between last year and this year. I thought of the changes and variables that may have affected the outcome. I tried to analyze the data and understand it. In the end, I identified an objective explanation, which satisfied me and led me to make a commitment to myself: I'll try this again in the future. I will swim that event again; I will do it again when I feel better; I will try it again when I don't have other things on my mind besides the goal I want to reach. I am sure that next time, in the conditions I will establish for myself, the record will not elude me because there is nothing that I cannot achieve if I believe in myself. There is no unexpected situation that may become a defeat because defeats are for losers. And if it were to happen that I may not obtain what I desire, I am sure that I will always know how to put myself in a condition to say, "As always, this time I played a good game. As always, I put my heart and soul in it. As always, I lived every moment of my life most intensely and uniquely. I am happy for this. Because no matter how it goes, in the end what matters is that I will always be proud of myself."

EMOTION
My friend Alberto

Alberto was born on March 27, 1965, exactly eight years before me, not a day earlier, nor a day later. For about twenty years, he led a normal life, made of friends, school and various hobbies. His parents own a house on Lake Maggiore, so he often spent the weekends contemplating that charming body of water that shined under his eyes. He was still a child when he heard the news that will change his life: that lake, exactly that section that he knew so well was crossed by a swimmer 15 years older than him! Alberto was blown away; that guy became his hero, his point of reference and a role model to emulate. His imagination began to gallop, feeding ever more creative and red-hot wishes.

In the summer of '84, at the age of 19, Alberto turned to action. While riding his inflatable mattress during an afternoon swim in the lake waters in front of Stresa, he remembered the endeavor that that boy had pursued years earlier. Playing around, he began to row toward the middle of the lake and, not fully grasping how quickly he could move, he traveled a few hundred meters. Not too far from him, aboard a boat, his brother curiously watched him; then, realizing what Alberto was doing, his brother began to follow him. Within a few minutes, the air mattress traveled very far, and his passenger was convinced that he could float to the opposite shore of the lake. After 4 kilometers of rowing and feeling pleasantly surprised with himself, Alberto reached the other side. He didn't know it yet, but it was already written in the stars. His appetite for adventure had been aroused... and now his stomach claimed an all-you-can-eat meal!

The following year, he signed up for a skydiving course and on April 14, 1985, he performed his first jump. Aboard a small airplane with no hatch and with his shoulder hanging outside the plane for the entire trip, Alberto gave one last look at that soccer field that had shrunk to the size of a stamp and he jumped out at an elevation of 600 meters in extremely loud conditions. A few seconds later, his parachute deployed and the noise made way for silence. Alberto enjoyed the view and was almost moved by the beauty he witnessed.

If you asked him why he wanted to do something like that, he would frown, turn doubtful and give you no answer. He would tell you that maybe this is one of those dreams that grow inside you when you are a child, or maybe that this is the thrill of having a slightly unusual experience. The thing is: he liked it.

Months went by and summer arrived at the end of the school year. His friends decided to go to Tuscany, so he went with them. His friends drove, while he decided to ride his bicycle. There is nothing wrong with that; in the end, there are loads of people who do stuff like that and ride bicycles all over Europe. The point is that Alberto decided to do that at the drop of a hat, all of a sudden and without ever having trained or ridden any considerable distances. However, by now his mind was made up. On the morning of his departure, he was in his storage shed with his father: he climbed on his bicycle and his father got in the car to go to work. Their gazes crossed; then the parent lowered his window to pronounce the most encouraging phrase anyone could say to his children: "Son, you are nuts!"

Alberto pedaled along happily. He arrived in Voghera and called home to reassure his mom, who, like all moms, could not help but worry about his son doing such crazy bravado. He spent his first night on the beach in Genoa, the second night on the beach in San Terenzo, the third night at a campground in Follonica and then, on the morning of the fourth day, as if his were a biblical voyage, he reached his destination, wrapping up his ride in three and one-half days. At the end of his vacation, Alberto's life returned to normality.

Alberto works as an IT programmer, creating computer software. He uses technology every day to create virtual objects that exist only when the machine is on and, when the machine is turned off, the fruit of his labor vanishes. Maybe that is why he constantly seeks contact with reality through physical effort and contemplation of nature. Or maybe the fact that his creations are used by others makes him want to create something that remains only his. The fact is that when Alberto takes on a challenge, he feels alive and at peace with the world.

It was the summer of 1987. Also that year, Alberto decided to go on vacation with his friends. Also this time he wanted to reach the others using an alternative mode of transportation. Too bad this year's destination was Tropea, located in the southern region of Calabria and the means he chose to reach that destination was roller skates! The extraordinary fact is that Alberto had never skated in his life. He bought skates purposely to make the trip; then, just to be certain, he tried them on a few days before setting out and, after having fallen to the ground about twenty times, he took them off saying to himself, "1300 kilometers will be more than enough distance to learn." On the day of his departure, he packed a backpack with eight pairs of spare rollers. He began skating down the road behind his house, falling repeatedly. He soon realized that this was not working. His fears centered on Via Emilia, a state route where cars and trucks zoom by at fast speeds and where falling down would be a really bad thing. Before even reaching the nearby town of San Donato Milanese, Alberto turned around, went home, removed his roller skates and hit the road on foot. He calculated that, if he walked 80 kilometers a day, he should arrive in Calabria just in time to enjoy some vacation. After walking for five hours and covering "only" thirty kilometers, his feet began to bleed profusely. He entered into the city of Lodi and, without hesitating he headed for a cycle shop to buy a bicycle. He looked around dreamingly; then he counted the money he had in his wallet and had to settle for a used bicycle with broken wheels, galloping rust and hiccupping breaks. Besides that, the wreckage seemed capable of moving. Alberto placed his backpack on the handlebars, tied it down with a rope wrapped around the seat, climbed on the bike and started pedaling until he reached the Cisa Pass. His legs began feeling heavy and the bicycle gears refused to engage. Alberto got off the bike and walked up what felt like a never-ending hill. Once he reached 800-meter elevation, he felt dazed with fatigue and it took a few seconds for him to understand the meaning of the following sign, "Berceto: the mountain community closest to the sea." Lastly, he climbed back on the bike and started down the longest downhill path of his life, from Cisa to Aulla. He sat on his bike without pedaling for so long that he almost thought he was riding a moped, but he soon realized that the party was over and it was time to start pedaling again. He traveled through Lunigiana, Maremma and along the Tyrrhenian coast. In Cecina, with the sun beating down on his head, he stopped at a public phone booth to call home, but he had to cut it short due to a sudden unexpected meltdown of sweat. He traveled through empty roads, gorgeous locales, hot settings and more temperate climates. After fifteen days on the road, two of which spent resting, he reached Tropea, where a new unexpected situation awaited him: as he pulled over to take a selfie of himself standing under the town sign, he ran into the sidewalk, breaking three spokes. After snapping his picture, he put his backpack over one shoulder, his bike over the other shoulder and completed the last seven kilometers on foot, feeling like Rambo.

Despite the fatigue, the heat, and the pain that he might have felt in his legs and buttocks, the only thing that Alberto truly felt during his trips was a profound sense of inner peace that gave him the strength he needed to press on, although he was not adequately ready. Maybe it was during this last leg that he discovered his own motto, that statement that captured me when I listened intently to his tales and that I defined "Alberto's steak approach." Try to imagine that you have a one-inch-thick steak as large as a pizza under your nose. It looks very much like the one devoured by Fred Flintstone in the cartoon "The Flintstones." Sitting in front of a similar plate, you and I would probably say, "I definitely could not finish anything that large," as if we had to swallow it all up in one gulp. On the other hand, Alberto would say, "Well, little by little, small piece by small piece, bite after bite, I can finish it

without any problems." Because he is like that; he is not afraid when he is faced with something enormous: he admires its beauty and it makes his mouth salivate. Then, with placidness, he faces the challenge confident that he can complete it, even though he has never tried doing that before.

Filled with this type of mental strength, on Sunday July 14, 1991, at the age of 26, after buying a brand new bicycle and loading his bag, tent and sleeping bag, Alberto took off toward North Cape to complete a 4,000-kilometer ride. On the first day, he completed 80 kilometers and arrived dead tired at Belizean. He took a shower, had a light meal and a little rest. The next day, thinking that, "you don't need to be a champion to cruise at 20 km an hour," he continued its journey. He crossed Switzerland and then Germany, proving how practice can quickly improve strength and endurance.

Ten days after he took off from Milan, traveling an average speed of 160 km a day and having covered a total route of 1,600 kilometers, he arrived in Copenhagen, where the unexpected happened. For the first time in one of his trips, Alberto felt discouraged. It had been ten days since he had spoken to anybody and, as his girlfriend was too far to give him comfort, his ride began feeling like too tough a challenge for his heart and mind. As it happens in these cases, divine providence intervened to fix things. While he sat alone on a bench of a nameless square in Copenhagen, staring at the empty space and holding a sandwich that was too flavorless to be fully enjoyed, he realized that, next to him, sitting on another bench, was a couple in their fifties which was looking at him. They initially hesitated, but then they approached him and, speaking broken English, asked him to take a picture. It didn't take him long to realize that they were Italians and he soon found out that they came from Mariano Comense. After taking their picture, Alberto, who finally had someone to talk to, shared what he was trying do. Their eyes opened wide; they praised him and made him feel like a hero. It was just what he needed! Once again, he climbed on his bike and took off like a champ. He took the ferry and arrived in Sweden. His pedals began feeling very light, so much so that he completed the last 2,400 km in only ten days. The training effects of the first half of the trip were yielding all their benefits.

His typical travel day involved waking up at seven, taking off at eight, taking a one-hour break for lunch and then go for another pedaling session. In the evenings, as he rested at his hotel, he spent most of his time setting up the next day's route, compiling an infinite series of notes including the most absurd directions (in 1991 navigators were still sci-fi). In his heart, he nurtured the dream of becoming a star of something beautiful and important, even more so when blessed with unrepeatable weather conditions (in twenty-two days, it only rained twice). His eyes were filled with an ever more challenging landscape, images that, in his mind, turned into motivational energy for his body, which received all it needed to push those small pedals ever harder. When he realized that he had put 3.000 kilometers behind him, Alberto convinced himself even more that his endeavor was nearing a conclusion. He rode over 2,000 kilometers through Sweden, encumbered just once by a flat tire.

Every time a gas station attendant, a fellow cyclist or any resident of the area asked him where he came from and where he was going, Alberto told them in his naturally sincere tone and receiving responses filled with oohs and aahs, raised eyebrows and enormous smiles. When he saw the sign "North Cape, 500 kilometers to go," Alberto couldn't wait to get there. He started feeling like he just needed to turn the corner and he would soon be there. At sixty-six degrees latitude, in shorts and bare-chested, he rode for 60 kilometers without running into a soul, which oddly led him to deep reflection on the meaning of life and the unavoidability of death. The only lively moment he encountered was in the company of about twenty reindeer, which played with him by letting him chase them for a while after meeting in the middle of the street. Compared to two weeks earlier, Alberto was a different man: he went from weighing 187 to 163 pounds, although his diet had doubled in all the food groups. On August 4, he rode the last 33 kilometers along a dirt road. Twenty days after his departure from Milan, after riding his bicycle for 4,000 kilometers, experiencing moments of fatigue and mental exhaustion, solitude and excitement, Alberto, feeling infinite joy matched by only that felt by the first man to set foot on the Moon, rested his tired feet at North Cape.

I tried asking Alberto what he remembered of his arrival, which was maybe the most spectacular achievement of his life. As usual, first he kept quiet, then he smiled at me and, after moving his eyes up and down a couple of times as if he were selecting the images and emotions to put into words, he looked at me and stopped himself in his tracks. After what seemed to be an endless pause, he laughed and changed the subject, telling me of three other Italians who also arrived at North Cape that day: two from Varese by car

and one from Turin, who, before meeting Alberto, felt like a hero for having ridden his motorcycle all the way. Alberto's own uncle, a convinced biker, would later tell Alberto, "I too wanted to ride my motorcycle to North Cape... but what's the point now?!?"

In September Alberto received the most amazing gift: dinner with Walter Bonatti, the world-famous Italian mountaineer. A common friend, galvanized by Alberto's story, had no difficulty setting up the meeting, during which Alberto was praised by Walter. For a moment, Alberto's head spun: he is a great fan of Bonatti's so he felt like, for a moment, the world had turned upside down.

1991 was a special year for Alberto because, after taking a long break from swimming, he managed to return to the pool and swim his 3000 meters in lap swim. Two years later, at the age of 28, he tried to take a major step in his life and attempted to become a professional helicopter pilot. He received his private pilot's license after accumulating the necessary 40 flight hours and having spent a fortune. This was 1993, and spending 500 thousand lira on an hour of flight was no easy thing to do. So, twenty-two million liras later (the amount included the flight hours, educational materials and the instructor hours), Alberto was told that, before he could continue his journey to the next step, that of earning a "commercial" pilot's license to transport people, he must undergo routine medical testing, administered by the Italian Air Force in Milan. Their verdict was cold: light color blindness detected, therefore Alberto was declared unfit to fly. Alberto's delusion hit him hard, but he was not devastated, maybe because the presence of his girlfriend Gabri, who had been by his side for a while now, had made him stronger and capable of continuing to withstand heavy blows.

In the summer of 1993, he experienced the most beautiful vacation of his life, thanks to Gabri. While hugging each other, they jumped down from a height of 103 meters, hanging from a bungee cord somewhere in France. Then, they rode their bicycles for 1,670 kilometers over two weeks, taking in the amazing countryside and castles of the Loire valley.

This cycling journey convinced the couple to try, two years later, to cycle around Iceland, an endeavor that they could not complete due to apocalyptic environmental conditions, to say the least: they ran into darkness, wind, rain and cold! After a most arduous leg of 140 kilometers and with his partner in tears due to the unbearable conditions, Alberto decided to hang their bikes on the rack of a bus and use motorized transport to explore what he defined as "the most unreal place on Earth."

Then it was a new year, a new vacation and a new extravagant idea. This time, Alberto wanted to swim around the island of Elba (a total distance of 120 kilometers). Gabri was the person who could make it all happen for him, giving him the necessary support on board a canoe. What's wrong with that? Well, Gabri did not know how to sail a canoe. So what was his solution? Get to the island a week earlier, take canoe paddling lessons and then begin the swimming adventure. Once they arrived on the island, they realized that winds and currents were too unpredictable to set out on a canoe: a small distraction could lead dangerously astray. To avoid putting his partner at risk, Alberto gave ups his endeavor, granting himself a week of the most absolute relaxation at the beach.

In 2003, at the age of 38, Alberto's life was shaken up once again. He began working at a different location, returned to attending the pool and began working hard at swimming laps. Every day at noon, he swam back and forth until Lorenzo, a fellow swimmer who had been observing him for days, stopped him to ask what the heck he was trying to prove by dragging himself through the pool like that. A moment later, Alberto joined Lorenzo's training group, thus beginning his chase for the best swimming performances of his life.

After continued workouts of 50, 100, 200 and 400-meter repetitions and training five times a week for an average for 4-5 kilometers, Alberto went from initially weighing 194 pounds to 154, getting slim and buffed. He proudly recalls how he could swim 100-meter freestyle in 1 minute and eight seconds.

Then, on that cursed March, 22, 2004, five days before his thirty-ninth birthday, at six o'clock in the morning, while riding his bicycle to work along the Pullese State, his lane was occupied by a car that slammed right into him; it was a drunk driver. The impact was extremely violent. By a twist of fate, Alberto was flown by helicopter to the hospital. Having recovered from his coma and multiple fractures, he realized that his body had lost part of its mobility: one of his ankles was in bad shape, he lost his cruciates in one knee and he was missing half a pinkie.

He spent several months in the hospital, sometimes undergoing 7 hours of physical therapy a day to break the adhesions that blocked one leg and to restart a set of movements minimally compatible with an active lifestyle. In these conditions, Alberto took an important decision: he got married. On that day, he left the hospital, went to the pool to swim, went to city hall to get married and then returned to his hospital bed.

Swimming is a great medicine, although training for 6 kilometers alternating one lap of freestyle and one lap of backstroke is not the best thing to do, especially when you have a leg that sticks out of the water as a pole when you do your flip turn.

Thanks to its "small bites" approach, Alberto successfully swallowed even this most bitter steak. Sure, there are some things he can no longer do (he had to give up mountain climbing), but there are many others that he still has not done and they are still out there, waiting to be savored...

Swimming is the sport that Alberto practices the most, for obvious reasons. In 2006, while talking with some pool patrons, he discovered the existence of open water events and, more specifically, that a crossing would be held right by his house on the lake. For a moment, he remembered the endeavor by that boy who was 15 years older than him and convinced himself that now was the time to imitate that role model whom he had never forgotten. He signed up, participated and completed the 3.3 km in a time of 59 minutes and 49 seconds. He enjoyed the experience so much that he personally pledged not to miss any future events. But, things got worse before they could get better and, in 2008, he fell from his motorcycle and broke one rib. He considered skipping the next crossing, but then his buddy told him, "What's with a broken rib? They worst that can happen is that you'll feel pain; your rib won't come off, you know!" So Alberto decided to participate anyway, going down in history as "the swimmer with the broken rib."

In 2008 the pool where he trained changed management and the quality of the facilities dropped. Alberto began going to a different pool and joined a master's swim team, mine. At the first practice of the season, I welcomed him as if he was a first-time customer and, with great enthusiasm, I told him all about how we train and how we work our master's level meets. I suggested consulting my website to get additional information. In my blog, because that's what it is, I have fun recounting the semi-serious events of my endeavors. Alberto enjoyed reading my stories. He read them all, including my old ones in the archives and there he encountered the dossier on my first Iron Master. The latter struck a chord with him. He decided that he wanted to experience the exact same thing and in the same desperate conditions, as he only knew how to swim two strokes out of four (his biggest challenges being butterfly and breaststroke).

From January to June, Alberto completed two whole Iron Masters: one in short-distance and one in long-distance pools. What is most amazing is that, among so many events, he also managed to participate in a water marathon. On March 2009, Alberto, without special training, went to Zurich for a 12-hour swim alone, which he took on as two sessions of approximately 6 hours each, separated by a rest cycle of forty-five minutes. When he got out of the pool, besides vomiting here and there, he celebrated having completed a swim distance of 28.9 kilometers. Mauro Giaconia, a world record holder who, a few months earlier, had swum 101 kilometers over 24 hours in Chile, congratulated him.

Alberto began pursuing a million swimming endeavors. With his approach of eating a steak bite after bite, in the period from July to September he put together eleven lake crossings and a Sicily Cup swim event at sea. The latter was especially challenging because, in addition to the effort of swimming 24 kilometers over four days, he had to bear the pain caused by being stung by as many as thirteen jellyfish.

In October, he returned to swim marathons, this time participating in a 24-hour event in Austria, obviously without special training. The environmental conditions were pushing the limit. The outdoor pool was constantly pounded by incessant rain; the water temperature was only 24°C, while the outside temperature was 1°C. Not wearing any diving gear, but thinking that he must also savor this steak bite by bite, he ended up swimming 47.8 kilometers during this competition.

This time Alberto felt the pain. He confided that, unlike when you ride a bicycle, which allows you to admire nature and maintain your mental energy while you pedal, keeping your sanity in a pool at two o'clock in the morning, when all you can see is a black line on the floor requires an insane effort.

In 2010, at the age of 45, Alberto repeated the 12 hours of Zurich, the Iron Mater and a good amount of crossings. But he wouldn't be Alberto if he wouldn't add something new. This time it was called Triathlon and the distance was none other than the most extreme there is: the Iron Man. The competition required that athletes first swim 3.8 kilometers, then ride their bicycles for 180 kilometers and, lastly run for 42 kilometers. All events must be completed on the same day in a maximum time of 16 hours. While the world's best triathletes can complete it in approximately 8 hours, Alberto hoped to finish before the judges stopped him, which was something he feared as he was totally untrained for the running event.

He began the race. After getting through the swimming and cycling events, barely completed by the time limit, Alberto took on the running event by walking. His ankle, which he had injured in his accident, bothered him. He ignored it and, from time to time, he even ran a little. After covering a little over 30 kilometers and after 16 hours from the beginning of his event, Alberto was stopped by judges for having exceeded the time limit. As a response, he returned home, visited the event's website and signed up for the 2011 edition, promising his friends, "This time I swear I'll train."

EXERCISE

Try to answer the following questions.

Which sports goals would you like to achieve?

What would it mean for you to achieve these goals?

What are the obstacles that currently keep you from achieving your goals?

How important are your dreams to you?

If you achieved your sports goals, would you feel like an important part of your life has come to fruition?

CHAPTER 11: EPILOGUE

Ten years of swimming have transformed me into a true athlete. After attending instruction courses for the first four years, during the last six years of masters swimming, I collected 168 individual competitions, three Iron Masters, three relays, seven crossings, two Italian Championships and one European Championship. Whether these numbers are extraordinary or plane ordinary, these are the numbers that define my experience in sports, an experience which, in addition to making me proud of myself, produced the effect of reprogramming my head and changing me physically as well as spiritually, making me stronger and more convinced that I can take on and win my challenges. Whatever those may be…

Ever since I began swimming competitively, I have never participated in any competitions during the month of September, on one hand because the masters swimming calendar does not hold any competitions that month and, on the other hand, because the rest accumulated during the month of August does not pair up well with the adrenaline rush needed to compete in any event. However, this year I felt like doing something different, so here I was, sitting on a bench along the boardwalk of Marina di Pisa; it was nine AM on Sunday, September 5. I looked around for my eyes to meet other wondering eyes, but, at this time, I couldn't see any. Bored and a bit resigned, I was killing time

observing the organizers' activities, who were taking their time (the competition will begin at eleven) to set up awnings and gazebos to make sure everything was ready to go. For a moment, I thought that I could go to the beach and sunbathe next to Claudia, but the idea of possibly getting dehydrated ahead of time led me to abandon the idea, feeling a bit terrorized.

Time went by and the place began to gradually become livelier. As stated in the schedule, the "changing area" opened at ten o'clock: this was a fenced off area of the square inside which the organizers set up tubular stalls lined up in parallel rows for athletes to "hang their clothes..." or, at least that's what I think. To understand what I was supposed to do in there, I let in a couple of people before me and then, with ill-concealed indifference, I follow them and watched what they did. Once I thought I understood the purpose of the stalls, I headed for the one labeled with my bib number. I pulled cap and goggles out of my duffel bag and placed them extremely carefully on the ground. Not satisfied with my results, I picked up my cap and rolled it up so I could put it on in no time. At this point, I closed my eyes and tried to visualize what I would be doing in one-half hour: *"After running one and one-half kilometers along the boardwalk, I will enter the changing area, grab cap and goggles and take off my shoes. Then, I will run to the wharf and, from there, I will dive in and swim for 750 meters. Next, I will exit the water and run again for one last kilometer."* My mental visualization of this Aquathlon race led me to think that it will not feel as excruciating as swimming 200 meters of butterfly, or at least it shouldn't be as demanding as the "standard" events of Triathlon, which normally include a swimming event, a cycling event and a running event. I mentally went over everything I must do and I adjusted my plan considering my current physical shape. All of a sudden, my positive approach began to feel a bit uncertain: will my swims in open waters and the six running training sessions put together to prepare for the 10-kilometer Stralugano race at the end of the month be enough? It was no use to try to find an answer...no use now, at least! When I felt like I had done enough visualizing, I opened my eyes and began my warm-up, getting ideas from what the others were doing. Were they flinging their legs? I would do that too. Were they practicing their sprints? I would follow them. I completed every copying action with extreme discretion, avoiding that those I was "observing" may realize what I was doing.

Around 11 o'clock, the announcer called all participants to the start line. Here we go. I began to feel the adrenaline in my stomach; however, instead of feeling charged, this time I felt relaxed and I was having fun. In the end, I was just a slightly experienced beginner surrounded by a group of fierce triathletes, therefore my objective was just to complete the race and get a good time in the swim event. To avoid bothering others during the start of the race, I stood behind the forty participants as I was certain that I could not keep up with their pace. At the start signal, everyone sprinted as if their race consisted of 100 meters, rather than 1,500. As I had a vague feeling that I would not catch up to them, I let them get away. At the turn by the buoy, the group looked definitely stretched out, so much so that, at the end of the first running event, despite my efforts and the fact that my heavy breathing could be heard from outer space, I placed among the last few. I entered the change area, took off my shoes, picked up my cap and goggles and ran toward the sea, trying to put on everything on the run. As I carefully and decidedly chased the others, I dove in, brushing against a fellow competitor. When I entered the water, my body shivered, but this only lasted for a fraction of a second and it was forgotten as soon as I felt the disgusting taste of salt on my mouth. I began to swim, having trouble breathing and unusually feeling like I was dragging my arms. I gathered all the lucidity I could muster to make myself stretch out my stroke, swimming slowly and relaxingly. I succeeded in doing exactly what I wanted, because I reached and pass various competitors, who were swimming by slapping their arms disorderly. At the turn by the buoy, I realized that I was only at the halfway point and that my energy was almost entirely used up. I looked for a mental image that could restore the energy I needed, but now reality set in where my imagination struggled: in front of me appeared another set of feet belonging to other competitors to pass. I gathered my strength, intensified the action and passed a few more swimmers with determination. I exited the water and stood up. I felt a bit light headed: I grinded my teeth, muffled my staggering and reached the changing area. When I reached my stall, I removed cap and goggles, put on my shoes and took off again for the last kilometer of running. The first one-hundred meters felt easy, the second one-hundred were a bit more challenging, but when I got to three-hundred, everything got more complicated as I began feeling pain around my liver. I slowed down. Two of the competitors I passed while swimming caught up to me. When I finally reached the finish line, it came as a natural instinct to look up to the sky, take a deep breath and laugh for the great satisfaction I felt. My arms were shaking. I looked for Claudia's happy face; when our eyes found each other, I gave her an immense smile. As a response, she touched her forehead. She now realized that my adventure into the world of triathlon had just begun...

... but this, my dear friend, is another story.

MY PERSONAL RECORDS
(SO FAR)

EVENT	TIME
50FR	0'28"94*
100FR	1'06"50
200FR	2'30"73
400FR	5'25"60
800FR	11'46'32
1500FR	23'14"60
50BK	0'38"29
100BK	1'22"13
200BK	2'56"13
50BR	0'39"90
100BR	1'30"87
200BR	3'26"18
50FL	0'35"08
100FL	1'34"23
200FL	3'49"36
100MED	1'20"95
200MED	2'59"11
400MED	6'38"74

*50-meter pool

Printed in Great Britain
by Amazon.co.uk, Ltd.,
Marston Gate.